KARL BARTH IN PLAIN ENGLISH

STEPHEN D. MORRISON

BELOVED PUBLISHING · COLUMBUS, OH

eBook ISBN: 978-1-63174-158-6

Paperback ISBN: 978-1-63174-159-3

Cover illustration and design copyright © 2017 Gordon Whitney Media (www.GordonWhitneyMedia.com)

Beloved Publishing · Columbus, Ohio

Second edition: April, 2018.

Acknowledgments

First and foremost I want to thank my dear wife, Ketlin, for graciously putting up with my many long-winded theological ramblings, for being a constant source of inspiration and encouragement, and for ultimately giving me the courage to pursue my dreams. I'd be half the man I am today if not for you!

Several reviewers were kind enough to offer helpful, constructive criticism on the content of this book. My thanks to John Moore, Ian Gilchrist, Neil Colombé, and David Tralaggan; your comments were much appreciated.

I also want to thank Gordon Whitney, not only for your excellent illustration of Barth and your cover design but for your friendship, which I am constantly grateful for.

And finally, I want to thank the Karl Barth Discussion Group on Facebook, which has been a constant source of engaging dialogue around Barth's theology. I've enjoyed learning with you all, and I look forward to continuing to learn with many of you in the years to come.

CONTENTS

PREFACE

This is a book for beginners, by a beginner, on the theology of Karl Barth. The aim is to offer a clear and precise presentation of Barth's thought, without the complicated theological jargon often involved in discussions about his work. This book strives for simplicity without oversimplification, clarity without skimming over the details, and brevity without lacking in depth. I hope to present a fair and accessible look into Barth because I believe his work deserves a wider audience, not just among the "professionals" but among us "amateurs" too.

I am an amateur, and I am not afraid to admit it. I don't have the traditional qualifications for writing a book like this, but that is precisely why I wrote it. I don't hold a degree in theology, nor do I understand Latin, Greek, or even German! And yet, I believe Barth's work *should* be accessible to others who, like me, also lack these qualifications. I hope this book encourages other amateurs to take up the challenge; because if *this* amateur can make his way through Barth's work and learn a great deal from it still, then so can you. At the very least—even if you decide *not* to read Barth on your own after reading this book—I hope you gain a clearer understanding of Barth's theology in the midst of so much *mis*understanding circulating about it today.

Finally, I'm honored that you've picked up *my* little book, over all the other big or small books on Karl Barth, and I do hope you put it down with a better appreciation of his theology. But that is not my only hope. Ultimately, I hope you walk away with your eyes more firmly fixed on the person of Jesus Christ and His gospel of exceedingly great joy.

STEPHEN D. MORRISON
COLUMBUS, 2017

INTRODUCTION

Imagine an enormous mansion at the end of a road, guarded by an intimidating row of gigantic trees, with its gate wide open. Now imagine one day you find in yourself the courage to investigate this daunting house, walking right through the gate, across the garden, and through the front door. You suddenly find yourself in a *labyrinth* made up of many rooms, of grand, gothic structures, of profound complexity and beauty. Everywhere you look, you are amazed at how much precision and care went into constructing the house; no detail has been left unattended. But then, in the midst of your explorations, you realize you have lost your way. You wish you were in a simpler house, one with fewer rooms and easier directions, even if it would be a house much duller in comparison.

Reading Karl Barth for the first time can make you feel like this: like you are stepping into a vast, confusing labyrinth. It can be easy to get lost, give up hope, and feel inadequate in the face of Barth's enormous body of work, his challenging prose, and his thoroughly complex mind. Indeed, if even the trained professional has difficulty navigating Barth, how much more difficult would it be for an amateur?

This book is my attempt, amateur to amateur, to be your guide through the labyrinth of Barth's theology. Because amateur or not, no one is disqualified in the Church of Jesus Christ from the pursuit of theology. As Barth reminds us:

In the Church there are really no non-theologians. The concept of 'layman' is one of the worst concepts in religious terminology, a concept that should be eliminated from the Christian vocabulary.

— GOD IN ACTION, 57

Every follower of Jesus Christ is invited to the task of theology—and not merely invited, but *called*. That does not mean every one of us will become professors or teachers, but we all should become *learners* confronted by God's Word in Jesus Christ. Barth argues that to study theology is not to become a "professional" theologian but to remain an *eternal student* of God's Word. He writes:

We are in a school from which we shall not some day be graduated in order to become masters ourselves. On the contrary, the school in which we are enrolled will make us increasingly students[.]

— GOD IN ACTION, 113

That is why Barth always reminded us to "begin again at the beginning" with God's self-revelation in the person of Jesus Christ. We will never master God's Word or turn it into *our* word; it remains *God's* free and gracious address to us. It is God's Word to humanity, and not humanity's word about God, which is the subject of theology. Therefore, this subject never becomes an object of our control. We are summoned by God's Word, to learn its content and, above all, know its Subject. Thus, we are *all* theologians in the Church.

To drive this point home, read this quote from one of Barth's final public addresses (on a radio show) where he made the startling claim that he is a layman:

I, too, am a layman. A layman is simply one who belongs to the people. All of us can only belong to the people—I mean, of course, God's people, which is all-embracing. [...] You are not to say to me: I am no expert in this matter, as though to say: it doesn't concern me. It concerns you just as much as it does me.

— FINAL TESTIMONIES, 35

Karl Barth's theology may be challenging, but it's not beyond the reach of those willing to work to understand it. Whether we are amateurs or professionals, we are *all* students at the feet of God's Word. With this spirit in mind, I, myself an "amateur" theologian, write this book to be your guide to one of the greatest modern theological minds of the twentieth century.

I hope you find in this book a precise and clear study of Karl Barth's theology and a helpful introductory overview of a few of his significant contributions. With this clarity and simplicity in mind, I do not wish to water down Barth but rather to make his work more accessible for those daunted or confused by him. For that reason, I am not presenting an exhaustive study of *every* minute point from Barth's entire work, which is far too large to cover in such a short, introductory book. Thus, a number of insights have been overlooked. Barth's major ideas, however, are all right here; the theological insights upon which Barth's reputation rests are present in this study.

Ultimately, I hope this book encourages you to pick up and read Barth for yourself, if you have not already begun that task, and to discover for yourself what Barth has to say. And moreover, I hope, with Barth, that this study does not lead you into a further fascination with Karl Barth the man from Basel, but with Jesus Christ!

Returning to our analogy of a house, my goal in this book is to introduce to you a few of the largest rooms, offer a few pointers on finding your way around, and then to leave you to discover on your own. After finishing this book, you are free to return to any room and stay as long as you like to study the details for yourself. Sometimes it can be helpful to have at your disposal an overview such as this one before you get too busy with the details of Barth's massive *Dogmatics,* his hundreds of sermons, his many letters, his essays and lectures, and his many other published works.

A BRIEF OUTLINE OF THIS BOOK

We'll spend the majority of this book exploring eight major ideas that I've chosen to focus on from Barth's theology. These are the ideas which I have personally found most helpful. For this, we will primarily rely on his *Church Dogmatics*. Here are the eight major ideas I've chosen from Barth's theology:

1. Barth's rejection of natural theology.
2. The Triune God of revelation
3. The "threefold" form of the Word of God: revelation, Scripture, and Church proclamation (preaching).
4. Barth's rejection of a hidden God behind the back of Jesus Christ.
5. The doctrine of election.
6. The doctrine of creation and the covenant.
7. The doctrine of reconciliation.
8. Barth's special theological emphasis on the Church and on ethics.

Here's how I've organized each chapter. First, I present a summary paragraph of the subject at hand. These summaries are a condensed version of each chapter, and they should not necessarily be considered a summary of Barth's complete thoughts on the matter. They are not an attempt to *contain* Barth's views on various issues, though they will act as helpful *guideposts* for understanding him better. John Webster was correct when he said, "Barth's views on any given topic cannot be comprehended in a single statement [...] what he has to say cannot be neatly summarized." (*Cambridge Companion to Karl Barth*, 9)

Second, I present a selection of quotes on each major idea. First, direct quotes in Barth's own words, and second, quotes by leading scholars of Barth's work.

Third, after the main text of each chapter, I conclude with a discussion of the *significance* of each major idea, which will immediately apply the practical ramifications of what we have just discussed.

In between chapters on each of these eight major ideas I have included several "sidebar" chapters. These serve to address contemporary issues, specific points of emphasis, or common misconceptions regarding what Barth is saying. These "sidebars" strive to clarify further Barth's insights, and they usually include an extended quote.

I also included small chapters with examples from Barth's sermons as they relate to each major idea. I've found Barth's preaching to be especially helpful for understanding his thought. These quotes are free from academic jargon, and place Barth's theology into an immediate and practical sphere—the sphere that Barth himself wanted his theology to be situated: the Church's proclamation in preaching.

So without further delay, let's dive in and discover more about Karl Barth and his theology.

BIOGRAPHY

Two things should be made clear from the start. First, when pronouncing Karl Barth's name, it is read "Bart" not "Barth." The "h" is silent. (Think "Bart" Simpson, not "bath" with an r thrown in the middle.)

It should also be clarified that Barth was not a German theologian; he was *Swiss*. Barth was born in Basel, Switzerland, and he lived there for most of his life. This misconception is likely from two sources. First, since Barth spoke and wrote in German (though he also knew French, English, Latin, and Greek) he is wrongly mistaken as a German; but this would be the same mistake as calling an American *British* because they speak English. Second, Barth was heavily engaged in German politics, which is probably the leading cause of the confusion. Barth was the primary writer of the Barmen Theological Declaration, an anti-Hitler statement of the Confessing Church, and this has often lead to the misidentification.

Karl Barth was born May 10, 1886, and died on December 10, 1968, at the age of eighty-two. He was the first-born son of Johann Friedrich ("Fritz") and Anna Katharina Barth. His father was, in his own right, a well-respected, conservative professor and theologian. Barth's childhood was spent in Bern, Switzerland, where his father was a New Testament and Church history professor.

In 1904, despite his father's conservative leanings, Barth spent his university years studying liberal theology. He began at Bern, then went on to Tübingen and Marburg (Germany). In Marburg, especially, Barth came under the influence of liberal theology as he studied with two of the most prominent liberal theologians at the time: Adolf von Harnack and Wilhelm Herrmann. Barth then served as a pastor in Geneva, preaching at John Calvin's Church for two years (1909-11), before spending ten years in the small town of Safenwil, Switzerland (1911-21).

It was in Safenwil, under the pressure of his pastoral duties to this predominantly blue-collar, working-class community, that Barth underwent his famous theological crisis. It was, first and foremost, a crisis of having something to say *about God*, as Barth later expressed so well:

> As ministers we ought to speak of God. We are human, however, and cannot speak of God. We ought therefore to recognize both our obligation and our inability and by that very recognition give God the glory.
>
> — THE WORD OF GOD AND THE WORD OF MAN, 186

Realizing both the *importance* and the *impossibility* of this task, Barth was forced to apply himself diligently, with his friend Eduard Thurneysen, to rediscover the "strange new world within the Bible." It was there in the small town of Safenwil that Barth wrote his first epoch-making book, *The Epistle to the Romans* (1919). This book was described best by Karl Adam, who said it fell "like a bombshell on the theologians' playground." It offered a fierce critique of liberal theology, and stressed the *Godness* of God, the God who is "wholly other."

On the strength of this work alone, Barth was invited to teach Reformed theology at the predominantly Lutheran University of Göttingen—despite the fact that Barth did not hold a doctorate. Barth developed a sincere appreciation for Calvin and Luther during this time, as well as for the Reformed tradition as a whole. This is what scholars sometimes refer to as Barth's "early" theology (often dated from 1910-1931).

Flannery O'Connor aptly captured the spirit of the "early" Barth in a letter, writing, "I like old Karl. He throws the furniture around" (*The Correspondences of Flannery O'Connor,* 180-1). There is nothing quite like the texts from this early period of Barth's career. Barth wrote with the sharp passion of a man who had freshly rediscovered the essential truths of our faith. "Well roared, lion!" was Barth's own response to his early work, in the *Church Dogmatics,* while commenting on an early passage in his *Romans* commentary (*CD* II/1, 635).

Barth moved from his position in Göttingen to Münster (1925-30), and then to Bonn (1930-35). Barth actively declared his opposition to National Socialism, even before Hitler's rise to power in 1933. In 1934, Barth helped write the Barmen Declaration, a theological declaration adopted by the Confessing Church in opposition to Nazi ideology. Barth even mailed the document directly to Hitler. Barth was active in the Confessing Church, together with Dietrich Bonhoeffer and several others. By refusing to begin his lectures with the customary "Hitler oath," Barth was forced to resign his teaching position and leave Germany (1935).

After the war, Barth would often visit Germany to give lectures and see old friends, but he would remain in Basel for the rest of his life. In Bonn, Barth had begun his *Church Dogmatics,* publishing volume I/1 in 1932. The remaining twelve volumes were written in Basel, with the indispensable help of his assistant, Charlotte von Kirschbaum. Barth retired from his position at the University of Basel in 1962.

Barth was fond of Mozart and even published a book of appreciation on the composer. He also enjoyed studying war history, riding horses, playing chess, and reading American detective novels. He lived an active and fruitful life, publishing numerous articles, lectures, essays, and books that in total more than double the length of his *Dogmatics*—which is already by itself twice the length of Aquinas' *Summa Theologica* and nine times the length of Calvin's *Institutes.* He was such a prolific writer that he once joked to a student (according to reports), "Even *I* haven't read everything I've written." It is difficult to put a number on just how much Barth wrote, but his productivity is staggering.

Karl Barth died in his sleep on the morning of December 10, after spending the evening listening to Mozart and writing yet another lecture. That lecture remained unfinished. His last written words abruptly end mid-sentence. What could be more testimonial to Barth's career than this incomplete sentence? He remained engaged his entire life, even in his later years, with so many social and political issues right alongside the theological issues of his time. His great work, the *Church Dogmatics,* likewise remains unfinished, but breathtaking still, like Gaudi's majestic Sagrada Família in Barcelona. It is this enduring faithfulness to the Word of God which makes Barth one of the most productive and inspiring theologians who ever lived.

Barth's life is fascinating, and essential for rightly understanding his work. We have only offered a brief look at the most significant events of his life. But I recommend for a thorough study of Barth's life to read Eberhard Busch's *Karl Barth: His Life from Letters and Autobiographical Texts.*

THE STRUCTURE OF BARTH'S CHURCH DOGMATICS

A few notes. First, Karl Barth's *Church Dogmatics* is abbreviated "*CD*" throughout this book. Second, page numbers are from the Hendrickson Publishers 2010 reprint edition. The citations from this edition faithfully correspond to the original T&T Clark 1956-75 edition, which is the current academic standard.

Additionally, please note that many of the quotations from Barth include non-gender-neutral phrases such as "man" or "mankind" instead of "humanity." This has *not* been corrected in direct quotes for the sake of clarity and consistency. But whenever we quote Barth, for example, discussing God's love for *man,* this does not mean God's love for *males.* Instead, take these instances in the more general sense of *humanity.* The same goes for Barth's tendency to use the pronoun "he" or "him" in the place of a general reference to people. This too is an inclusive rather than an exclusive term and should be understood as such. Likewise, as a tip for reading Barth, upper-case pronouns almost always indicate a reference to God or Jesus Christ. In the midst of Barth's long sentences, keeping that in mind can help find the proper reference point.

In this section, I want to present an outline of Barth's *Church Dogmatics.* This may be helpful as you begin reading Barth for yourself, because the topics covered in each volume are not always indicated very clearly, and it can be daunting to wade into the text without a map. This will also help you for reading this book, as we will refer to volumes of Barth's work. For example, *CD* IV/1, §60. This notation indicates volume four, "The Doctrine of Reconciliation," part-volume one, chapter fourteen, "Jesus Christ, the Lord as Servant," and paragraph sixty, "The Pride and Fall of Man." Most of the time I won't refer to paragraph numbers, but I always include a page number directly following the indicated volume and part-volume.

Barth's *Church Dogmatics* is made up of four volumes and thirteen part-volumes (plus an index). Barth did not live to write volume five, though he planned to address "The Doctrine of Redemption" (eschatology) in it. Volume four remains only partially complete, with just some of Barth's intended treatment of the Christian life and the ethics of reconciliation.

Volume one (I) is "The Doctrine of the Word of God" (two part-volumes: I/1, I/2). Volume two (II) is "The Doctrine of God" (two part-volumes: II/1, II/2). Volume three (III) is "The Doctrine of Creation" (four part-volumes: III/1, III/2, III/3, III/4). Volume four (IV) is "The Doctrine of Reconciliation" (four part-volumes, one of which is separated into halves: IV/1, IV/2, IV/3.1, IV/3.2, IV/4). Because Barth never wrote his "doctrine of redemption," volume five (V) indicates the index. This volume includes an aid for preachers.

CD is made up of sixteen "chapters" and seventy-three "paragraphs" (§). What follows is each of the chapter and paragraph headings for the entire work. I've added brackets for a few clarifications on the subject matter where it is not already apparent.

I/1 - The Doctrine of the Word of God
Introduction
§1 The Task of Dogmatics
§2 The Task of Prolegomena to Dogmatics
Chapter I: The Word of God as the Criterion of Dogmatics
§3 Church Proclamation as the Material of Dogmatics
§4 The Word of God in its Threefold Form
§5 The Nature of the Word of God
§6 The Knowability of the Word of God

§49 God the Father as Lord of His Creature

§50 God and Nothingness

§51 The Kingdom of Heaven, the Ambassadors of God and Their Opponents

III/4, THE DOCTRINE OF CREATION

Chapter XII: The Command of God the Creator

§52 Ethics as a Task of the Doctrine of Creation

§53 Freedom Before God

§54 Freedom in Fellowship

§55 Freedom for Life

§56 Freedom in Limitation

IV/1 - THE DOCTRINE OF RECONCILIATION

Chapter XIII: The Subject-Matter and Problems of the Doctrine of Reconciliation

§57 The Work of God the Reconciler

§58 The Doctrine of Reconciliation (Survey)

Chapter XIV: Jesus Christ, the Lord as Servant

§59 The Obedience of the Son of God

§60 The Pride and Fall of Man

§61 The Justification of Man

§62 The Holy Spirit and the Gathering of the Christian Community

§63 The Holy Spirit and Christian Faith

IV/2, THE DOCTRINE OF RECONCILIATION

Chapter XV: Jesus Christ, the Servant as Lord

§64 The Exaltation of the Son of Man

§65 The Sloth and Misery of Man

§66 The Sanctification of Man

§67 The Holy Spirit and the Upbuilding of the Christian Community

§68 The Holy Spirit and Christian Love

1

NEIN! TO NATURAL THEOLOGY

SUMMARY: Karl Barth rejected natural theology for the same reason the Apostle Paul rejected salvation by works: we cannot, as sinners, work ourselves up into salvation, so we also cannot, in the sinful knowing of our fallen minds, work ourselves up into the knowledge of God. God alone saves, and God alone reveals Godself. It is then Barth's rigorous dedication to the gospel of grace that stands behind his rejection of natural theology.

IN BARTH'S OWN WORDS:

One can *not* speak of God simply by speaking of man in a loud voice.

— THE WORD OF GOD AND THE WORD OF MAN, 196

The fact that we know God is His work and not ours. And the clarity and certainty in which we know Him are His and not ours. The possibility on the basis of which this occurrence is realised is His divine power.

— CD II/1, 40

It is by the grace of God that God is knowable to us.

— CD II/1, 70

Secondary quotes:

Natural theology is conceived as a theology according to which our access to God is not mediated but immediate, not miraculous but natural, and not unique in kind but generally given. [...] Natural theology assumes that we have some sort of independent and autonomous leverage with respect to grace. [...] It allows us to transform revelation from an unnerving if liberating question into an answer that we ourselves can control.

— George Hunsinger: How to Read Karl Barth, 96-7

No concept of God arrived at independent of the reality of Jesus Christ may decide what is possible and impossible for God. Rather, we are to say from what God as man in Jesus Christ is, does and suffers: 'God can do this.' For 'who God is and what it is to be divine is something we have to learn where God has revealed Himself and His nature'[.]

— Eberhard Jüngel: God's Being Is in Becoming, 99-100

The doctrine of the knowledge of God based on the analogy of being (*analogia entis*) affirms that since man and God share a like 'being,' man can arrive at some knowledge of God's being even apart from God's acts.

— David L. Mueller: Karl Barth, 90-1

Why begin here?

Why begin our study with Barth's rejection of natural theology? Why not another more essential doctrine such as election or the Trinity? For two reasons.

First, Barth's rejection of natural theology is perhaps one of the defining traits of his theology. Barth's No against natural theology is the launching point for many of his significant theological developments. From Barth's rejection of liberal theology to his doctrine of election—and with nearly every theological subject in between—the rejection of natural theology gives Barth's thought its unique shape. It would be an error to say that the foundation of Barth's entire theology rests on this one theme; Barth actively evades any such synthesis. For Barth, "[S]ystematic theology is a contradiction in terms" (*Evangelical Theology*, 180). However, Barth's theology does take much of its unique shape from this rejection of natural theology, and in some sense, his positive contributions are also the result of this rejection.

Second, Barth's rejection of natural theology is his most thorough and consistent polemical meditation. What I mean is, if there's one thing Barth argues *against* most passionately in his many books, it is natural theology. Any theologian wanting to develop a natural theology in the future will have to systematically wrestle with Barth's hundreds of pages dedicated to its rebuttal.

If natural theology were a building, then Barth has placed a bomb at its base. Anyone wishing to do theology in the future will have a choice to make: either to flip the switch and with Barth watch the whole infrastructure come tumbling down, or against Barth attempt to carefully diffuse the bomb. But no theology can ignore the ticking sound in the basement for very long; no theology after Barth can develop a natural theology as if nothing has happened.

Future theologians may wish to disagree with Barth, but they no longer have the luxury of *ignoring* him. Barth's contributions are far too significant, including his rejection of natural theology.

WHAT IS NATURAL THEOLOGY?

Barth defines natural theology as the attempt to know God apart from where God has given Godself to be known, that is, apart from God's self-revelation in Jesus Christ. Natural theology presupposes "a union of man with God existing outside God's revelation in Jesus Christ" (*CD* II/1, 168). In other words, natural theology goes behind the back of Jesus Christ by seeking a union with God, or some higher knowledge of God, independent of Jesus Christ. It is therefore akin to a rejection of grace and likened to (intellectual) salvation by works.

With this Barth also rejects a doctrine known as the *analogia entis,* the "analogy of being." Fundamentally, this is the doctrine that our *being* has an inherent *analogy* which corresponds to the being of God. Barth rejects this notion, writing, "We have no organ or capacity for God" (*CD* I/1, 168). We are not inherently capable of knowing God apart from God's gracious self-revelation.

By claiming that such an analogy exists, the doctrine of *analogia entis* asserts a "point of contact" between us and God, a neutral space in which we can know God apart from grace. Essentially, it claims that we might discover the knowledge of God someplace other than in Jesus Christ, whether it is in our self-consciousness, through logical deduction, or in the world God has made. For this reason, natural theology is sometimes known as a theology "from below." What Barth proposes, in contrast, is a theology "from above."

The analogy of being forms a basis for natural theology since it creates space for a theology arising out of our nature. The analogy of being, there-fore, provides natural theology with its foundation, namely, the possibility of knowing God *independent* of Jesus Christ. And that's the critical point, for Barth. The denial of Jesus Christ as the *only* revelation of God, as the only proper source of our knowledge of God, is what he finds most damnable about natural theology. For natural theology, speaking of God does not necessarily mean speaking exclusively of Jesus Christ, but for Barth, theology must only speak of God according to God's self-revelation.

Another difficulty with natural theology is, in Barth's view, how it ulti-mately creates an idol. In natural theology, we speak only about ourselves and have nothing to say about the true and living God. Just as an arrow shot into the sky must eventually fall back to the earth, so any notions of God we project onto God's nature from a basis in ourselves are ultimately only truths about *us* and not about God. In other words, it is an idol we create in our own image. The God attained by natural theology is always an idol.

Natural theology is fundamentally an *ungodly* and *unrighteous* attempt to know God apart from revelation. Barth writes in his commentary on Romans:

> Our relation to God is *ungodly*. We suppose that we know what we are saying when we say 'God'. [...] And our relation to God is *unrighteous*. Secretly we are ourselves the masters in this relationship. We are not concerned with God, but with our own requirements, to which God must adjust Himself. [...] God Himself is not acknowledged as God and what is called 'God' is in fact Man.
>
> — THE EPISTLE TO THE ROMANS, 44

When natural theology speaks of God, in truth, it plainly speaks of human beings in an elevated tone. The quotation from the beginning of this chapter offers the most lucid presentation of this idea. In a lecture on "The Word of God and the Task of Ministry," while discussing the errors of the theology of Schleiermacher, Barth said, "One can *not* speak of God simply by speaking of man in a loud voice" (*The Word of God and the Word of Man*, 196).

Schleiermacher's theology, according to Barth, placed human beings at its center, making knowledge of God equal with knowledge of ourselves. Barth was educated in this liberal tradition from his professors, but would later reject it so fiercely because he discovered that this speaking of God as man in an elevated tone is a false start; ultimately, it denies God the freedom to be God over and against human beings. Thus, Barth stressed the "wholly other" God in his *Romans* commentary.

Natural theology reduces theology to anthropology, that is, to the study of humanity. And this was the admission of the famous liberal theologian, Ludwig Feuerbach, when he said, "Theology *is* anthropology." But Barth refuses to reduce theology to a study of human beings because that would be a rejection of the grace of God to freely reveal Godself in Jesus Christ. We cannot go behind the event of God's self-disclosure, and therefore natural theology, in making such an attempt, must be rejected.

WHY DOES BARTH REJECT NATURAL THEOLOGY?

Ultimately, Barth's rejection of natural theology comes down to a passionate defense of the gospel of grace. Natural theology, which posits a natural capacity of sinful humanity to know God, acts as a kind of intellectual salvation by works. It is the attempt to reach God apart from, or even against, the person of Jesus Christ. It is an attempt to go behind the back of Jesus Christ, to find another point of contact with God and human beings—*another* union, *another* revelation, outside of Christ. Therefore, it is intellectual salvation by works, and Barth's No! to natural theology is at once a resounding Yes! to the gospel of grace.

Natural theology imagines a world where God's Word is not spoken *exclusively* in Jesus Christ and searches for other words which speak of God outside of Him. But if there is no salvation except through Jesus Christ, then there is also no revelation except through Him.

If we were to imagine salvation as an achievement by the sweat of our brow, then we would not only be mistaken theologians but poorly mistaken Christians. We know from Scripture that there is no natural analogy in our being with an inherent capacity for salvation. There is no alternative point of contact with which we can lift ourselves up into a right relationship with God. We are fallen, sinful human beings, paralyzed and dead in our flesh. God must come to us, must raise us from the dead; God must reach us in our estrangement, He must rescue and heal us. Salvation is wholly *God's work*. If we are saved, it is by grace alone through faith. That is the gospel. "For by grace you have been saved through faith, and this is not your own doing; it is the gift of God—not the result of works, so that no one may boast" (Eph. 2:8-9).

We would never imagine saving ourselves by works, but natural theology mistakenly presumes that we can know God in ourselves apart from grace. Is this not a kind of intellectual salvation by works? We know that we are sinners, wholly incapable of saving ourselves. We cannot raise ourselves from the dead; yet why would we pretend as if somehow our *intellect* is not also sinful and fallen, not dead? Why do we believe that our mind might somehow apprehend the knowledge of God by itself apart from grace?

Theology fails when it presupposes a neutral place, a point where our being and God's being correspond. Theology cannot be a theology of works; it must be a theology of grace. It *is* a human endeavor, but as such, it is an *impossible* task apart from God's gracious self-revelation.

Theology is not a free science in the sense that we can speculate however we wish about God. God refuses to be an object of human speculation. God confronts us with the Word of grace in Jesus Christ. Theology is *bound* and *controlled by* this Word. God reveals *God*; God discloses Godself to be known by us. Jesus Christ is God's *self*-revealing, His self-interpretation and witness. *Deus dixit*—God has spoken!

Barth's rejection of natural theology defends the freedom of the "wholly other" God over and against human beings. God is not under our control as if God were an apple in our hand that we could examine, study, and learn. God is free from our definitions, our speculation, and our attempts at knowing God by works. But in grace God has not remained an impossibility, God makes Godself known in Jesus Christ. In Him, we know God—but in Him alone. As Jesus explains in the gospel of Luke: "[N]o one knows who the Son is except the Father, or who the Father is except the Son and anyone to whom the Son chooses to reveal him" (Luke 10:22).

God's knowledge of Godself is a *closed* circle; it is inaccessible to us unless God acts graciously towards us, lifting us up to participate in God's knowledge of Godself. That is what we mean when we say that God reveals Godself in Jesus Christ: God's closed circle of knowledge is made open to us by grace through faith in Him. Natural theology attempts to make its way into that closed circle by works. It is thus a theological falsestart.

Significance: Barth's rejection of natural theology forces us to reexamine how we speak about God, reminding us that God has first spoken about Godself in Jesus Christ and it would be foolish to try and speak a different word other than *that* Word. Since God has spoken in this way, we are mistaken to speak about God in terms not bound to and controlled by Jesus Christ. A theology that begins with any such human analogy, starting with what *we* might imagine this highest and greatest being called "God" might be like, is at its core a form of idolatry. Barth's rejection of natural theology in this sense is a call to remember the first commandment, "You shall have no other Gods before me." And ultimately, it is a defense of the gospel of *grace*.

SIDEBAR: GOD'S HUMILIATION AND NATURAL THEOLOGY

To more clearly grasp Barth's rejection of natural theology, it will be helpful if we look at an example of how this works in more constructive terms. Here we'll briefly examine the way in which Barth discusses the *humiliation* of God in Jesus Christ from *CD* IV/1. Let's listen to what Barth has to say with the rejection of natural theology in mind:

> What [God] is and does He is and does in full unity with Himself. It is in full unity with Himself that He is also—and especially and above all—in Christ, that He becomes a creature, man, flesh, that He enters into our being in contradiction, that He takes upon Himself its consequences. If we think that this is impossible it is because our concept of God is too narrow, too arbitrary, too human—far too human. Who God is and what it is to be divine is something we have to learn where God has revealed Himself and His nature, the essence of the divine. And if He has revealed Himself in Jesus Christ as the God who does this, it is not for us to be wiser than He and to say that it is in contradiction with the divine essence. We have to be ready to be taught by Him that we have been too small and perverted in our thinking about Him within the framework of a false idea of God. It is not for us to speak of a contradiction and rift in the being of

God, but to learn to correct our notions of the being of God, to reconstitute them in the light of the fact that He does this.

— CD IV/1, 186

What is this contradiction? Plainly, it is the offense of the incarnation, the humiliation of God becoming a man in Jesus Christ. Natural theology would logically reject this event. The gods or our logical constructions could not become men or women, could not be as humble as they are exalted, could not suffer and die. Classical theism proves this is our natural inclination about God. We imagine that God cannot "become" anything, that God is the "unmoved mover," the impassible, unchanging, timeless, static (dead!) God.

But Jesus Christ shatters our preconceived notions of what God is like. Barth rightly reminds us that, "Who God is and what it is to be divine is something we have to learn where God has revealed Himself in Jesus Christ" (ibid). Natural theology presupposes a definition of God *before* discovering what God has revealed about Godself in Christ, and it thus attempts to fit the Word and works of God within its logic rather than discipline its logic according to God's Word and works. We can only learn of the incarnation, of God's becoming man for our sakes and suffering our contradiction—we can only learn this truth where God has taught it, in Jesus Christ. Looking to Christ and discovering what God has to say about Godself and is the only way for us to know God. The philosophical limitations we place on God cannot stand in the light of the incarnation.

Barth continues with who God is in the light of Jesus Christ:

> The mystery [of the incarnation] reveals to us that for God it is just as natural to be lowly as it is to be high, to be near as it is to be far, to be little as it is to be great, to be abroad as to be at home. Thus that when in the presence and action of Jesus Christ in the world created by Him and characterized *in malam partem* [as evil] by the sin of man He chooses to go into the far country, to conceal His form of lordship in the form of this world and therefore in the form of a servant, He is not untrue to Himself but genuinely true to Himself, to the freedom which is that of His

love. [...] It is His sovereign grace that He wills to be and is amongst us in humility, our God, God for us. But He shows us this grace, He is amongst us in humility, our God, God for us, as that which He is in Himself, in the most inward depth of His Godhead.

— CD IV/1, 193

Barth writes further on the lowliness of God which is at once God's majesty:

He is in and for the world what He is in and for Himself. He is in time what He is in eternity (and what He can be also in time because of His eternal being). He is in our lowliness what He is in His majesty (and what He can be also in our lowliness because His majesty is also lowliness). He is as man, as the man who is obedient in humility, Jesus of Nazareth, what He is as God (and what He can be also as man because He is it as God in this mode of divine being). This is the true deity of Jesus Christ, obedience in humility, in its unity and equality, its *homoousia,* with the deity of the One who sent Him and to whom He is obedient.

— CD IV/1, 204

The *way* Barth addresses this question of God's humiliation in Jesus Christ, of God becoming a man, is characteristic of his absolute rejection of natural theology. Moreover, this shows how diametrically opposite the conception of God in natural theology is over and against the God revealed in Jesus Christ. There is no synthesis. One is the god of human imagination, an idol: the object of natural theology. The other is the living Lord who reveals Godself in God's self-revelation: Jesus Christ.

WHAT IS POWER?

Think of how we classically define God's *power*. In natural theology, we imagine a God who is all-powerful, but we do so in such a way that God's power is, in reality, *our* definition of power *amplified* to the nth degree. But God's power cannot be defined by how we have misused the term. Power, in God's sense, is freedom. We imagine God's power to be an all-controlling, all-dominating force, like a cosmic dictator, but power for God is Jesus Christ in humiliation, suffering our condition to the point of death on the cross. God is *free* in God's power *to be weak*. God is free in God's authority to be humble and small, to be a crying baby in a Bethlehem manger. It is a paradoxical power, but this is what we confess when we declare God's victory in the defeat of the cross. In Christ's death, we say "Jesus is the victor!", and this alone shows how different the God of natural theology, which would never arrive at such a conclusion, is from the God of revelation.

G. C. Berkouwer notes this emphasis in Barth's thought, writing:

This conception of the true power of God constitutes one of the most essential elements in Barth's theology. It belongs not only to the doctrine of the attributes of God but—in connection with these—it has far-reaching significance for the doctrine of reconciliation. Here if anywhere we must remember that all of God's works can be seen only in the light of His revelation in Jesus Christ. We may not operate with 'general,' a priori ideas about God, as though we knew something about Him apart from His revelation. We must think about God exclusively in terms of Jesus Christ.

— THE TRIUMPH OF GRACE IN THE THEOLOGY OF KARL
BARTH, 125

Thinking of God exclusively in terms of Jesus Christ means rejecting natural theology as a false-start. This is Barth's "epistemological" No, and included in it is his Yes to revelation, which will be the subject of the next chapter.

SERMON: THE GREAT "BUT"

In an early sermon on Proverbs 16:2 Barth makes a helpful remark on natural theology. Proverbs 16:2 says, "All one's ways may be pure in one's own eyes, but the Lord weighs the spirit." This is an excellent text for understanding Barth's rejection of natural theology. Natural theology is that which we deem pure in our own eyes, the foundation we build in our own strength; yet there is this "great but" which stands between our self-made foundations and the only true foundation: God. God is the "great but" which contradicts all our attempts to work ourselves up into a knowledge of God with ourselves at the center. God confronts us as the God who may *not* be reached by what *we* deem pure, through our own works, but only as the God who makes Godself known to us by grace. God lives in unapproachable light, a light which must illuminate in our darkness, which we cannot reach by ourselves and must come to us by grace.

Barth writes:

> It is possible that whenever we utter the word 'God' we think of something high, great and beautiful, as a goal or ideal which we have set for *ourselves*. But fundamentally that would be a weighing of *ourselves* by *ourselves*; we ourselves would be our own judges and emancipate or condemn ourselves. But God dwells in a light

which no man can approach. Even the highest which we think about Him when measured by His true self is still an illusion. He alone accepts us or rejects us. He alone, He only. Wherever man stands before God he faces a 'Halt!' which he cannot escape, a 'Halt!' that can be compared only with death. Whatever belongs to our natural lives is not yet really of God. And what has come to us from God is no longer of us.

— COME, HOLY SPIRIT, 19-20

When we ourselves are the standard of measurement placed before God—when we imagine that whatever we deem pure stands up to what God deems pure—we only deceive ourselves. God stands as this "great but" in stark contradiction against our attempt to know God apart from the grace of Jesus Christ, to approach God's unapproachable light apart from God illuminating the darkness of our fallen mind.

2

THE TRIUNE GOD OF REVELATION

SUMMARY: God *reveals* God *through* God. We know God only *through* God and *in* God. Human beings cannot know God apart from God's self-revelation: Jesus Christ. God alone knows Godself. Only by grace through faith may we participate in God's knowledge of Godself. The subject of revelation is therefore identical with the event of revelation and the effect of revelation. God reveals Godself as the Divine "I" in threefold repetition: Revealer, Revelation, and Revealedness (i.e., the effect of revelation). We could also say Subject, Object, and Predicate; or finally, the Father, Son, and Holy Spirit.

IN BARTH'S OWN WORDS:

God is known only by God. God can be known only by God. At this very point, in faith itself, we know God in utter dependence, in pure discipleship and gratitude. At this very point we are finally dissuaded from trusting and confiding in our own capacity and strength.

— CD II/1, 183

Thus it is God Himself, it is the same God in unimpaired unity, who according to the Biblical understanding of revelation is the revealing

God and the event of revelation and its effect on man. …The doctrine of the Trinity is what basically distinguishes the Christian doctrine of God as Christian, and therefore what already distinguishes the Christian concept of revelation as Christian.

— CD I/1, 299, 301

Knowledge of God is then an event enclosed in the bosom of the divine Trinity.

— CD II/1, 205

SECONDARY QUOTES:

Revelation means God's self-interpretation as Father, Son, and Holy Spirit.

— EBERHARD JÜNGEL: GOD'S BEING IS IN BECOMING, 77

In Revelation God gives himself to us as the object of our faith and knowledge, but because he remains God the Lord, he does not give himself into our hands, as it were; he does not resign himself to our mastery or our control as if he were a dead object. He remains the living Lord, unqualified in his freedom, whom we can only know in accordance with his acts upon us, by following his movement of grace, and by renouncing on our part any attempt to master him by adapting him to our own schemes of thought or structures of existence; that is, [God is He] whom we can know only by knowing him out of himself as an objective reality standing over against us, as the divine Partner and Lord of our knowing of him. […] He reveals himself to us in such a way that we can know him only if our thinking begins with his revelation, and follows it through, if it is grounded entirely upon it, and never subjected to any other truth or criterion outside of it.

— THOMAS F. TORRANCE: KARL BARTH: AN INTRODUCTION TO HIS EARLY THEOLOGY 1910-1931, 82

Who can know God?

God knows Godself. God and *only* God knows God. If human beings know God, it is only through God's knowledge of Godself, by participating in that knowledge. Revelation is a *miracle* of grace. Since God in grace wills to make Godself known to us, God reveals God. God is the Revealer, the event of Revelation, and its effect, i.e., Revealedness. This Trinitarian structure of revelation refers back to the fact that God reveals Godself, not merely a part of God or a word about God, but that God indeed gives Godself to be known by us in Jesus Christ. The basis of our knowledge of God is by grace alone and in Christ's name.

Here we arrive at what many consider to be the heart of Barth's theology, his doctrine of revelation and the Trinity. Thomas F. Torrance writes in the editors preface to *CD* II/1, "Here we have the basis upon which the whole of Barth's teaching rests" (vii). Personally, if you asked me what the quintessential concept in Barth's theology is, I would have to say that it is this: *God reveals Godself.*

With the false possibility of knowing God through natural theology behind us, we now turn to the positive answer Barth gives to the possibility of Christian theology. In short, Barth argues the possibility of knowing God is only *God's* possibility, which only as such is gifted to human participants by grace through faith.

The first question Barth addresses in this regard is then not *our* knowledge of God, since we are forbidden to begin with ourselves or with humanity in general. Instead, we start with God. That is why we must first recognize that only God truly knows Godself, and if we participate in God's knowledge of Godself, then it is a secondary knowledge of God given to us only by grace. Barth writes:

> *Can* God be known? Yes, God can be known, since it is actually true and real that He is knowable through Himself. When that happens, man becomes free, he becomes empowered, he becomes capable—a mystery to himself—of knowing God. Knowledge of God is knowledge completely effected and determined from the side of its object, from the side of God.
>
> — Dogmatics in Outline, 24

Our knowledge of God is not in the first place *our* knowledge at all. It is God's knowledge of Godself. Barth stresses that we have no control over this knowledge, nor do we have any authority over it. This knowledge is "completely effected and determined from the side of its object." It is not *our* knowledge, primarily; by grace, we *participate* in God's knowledge of Godself.

The *how* of our knowledge of God is in the Pauline phrase: *by grace through faith*. Barth, in place of the analogy of being, argues for the *analogia fidei*, the analogy of faith. The fact that our knowledge of God is by grace through faith indicates that the object of our knowledge of God is never objectified in the sense that we have control over it, but it is always subjective, secondary, shared knowledge: God's knowledge of Godself. Faith participates through grace in this knowledge.

So the simplest answer, according to Barth, is that we know God because God wills to be known. In Jesus Christ, God has made Godself known. Therefore it is by grace, as God's gift, that we may know God. Theology is then bound strictly to the Word of God, to Jesus Christ. We cannot attempt to understand God apart from this grace, but only by participating through faith in God's very knowledge of Godself. In short, it is a *miracle* that we come to know God. As Barth writes:

> The Word of God becomes knowable by making itself known. [...] The possibility of knowing the Word of God is God's miracle on us just as much as is the Word itself or its being spoken.
>
> — CD I/1, 146

With Barth's rejection of natural theology, it became clear that in revelation we can never get behind Jesus Christ and seek after another source of revelation. Thus:

> We cannot get behind God—behind God in His revelation—to try to ask and determine from outside what He is. We can only learn and then attempt to repeat what He Himself alone can tell us and has told us—who He is.
>
> — CD II/1, 321

WHO IS THE SUBJECT OF REVELATION?

God is the subject of revelation. Therefore, we are confronted not merely with a word God wants to communicate *about* Godself, some piece of information about what God is like. No, Barth stresses the fact that in revelation we have to do with the very being of God as God is in Godself. Thus, the content of revelation is God: God in unimpaired unity and unimpaired distinction, God in Triunity. That is why the doctrine of revelation and the doctrine of the Trinity are so deeply intertwined in Barth's thought.

Barth's summary thesis of *CD* I/1 §8 is worth repeating in full:

> God's Word is God Himself in His revelation. For God reveals Himself as the Lord and according to Scripture this signifies for the concept of revelation that God Himself in unimpaired unity yet also in unimpaired distinction is Revealer, Revelation, and Revealedness.
>
> — CD I/1, 295

Another way of indicating this is when Barth says, "God is who He is in the act of His revelation" (*CD* II/1, 257). And again:

> God is who He is in His works. He is the same even in Himself, even before and after and over His works, and without them. [...] Yet in Himself He is not another than He is in His works.
>
> — CD II/1, 260

God's essential being is revealed in the person and work of Jesus Christ, in the acts of God towards us. The unity of who God is in Godself and who God is for us is a vital for Barth's doctrine of revelation.

In more classical terms, Barth stresses that the so-called economic Trinity (God for us) and the ontological Trinity (God in Godself) are inseparable. Who God is towards us in Jesus Christ, in the mighty acts of reconciliation and redemption, God is eternally and antecedently in Godself.

Eberhard Jüngel has argued that Barth's *Church Dogmatics* is a nothing less than a thorough exegesis of the statement, "God corresponds to Himself" (*God's Being Is in Becoming*, 36). And Thomas F. Torrance says the same thing in a different way when he writes:

> What God is toward us and for us in His revealing and saving acts [...] He is in His personal Being as Father, Son and Holy Spirit, and what He is in His personal divine being as Father, Son and Holy Spirit, He is toward us and for us in the revealing and saving acts of His.
>
> — THE CHRISTIAN DOCTRINE OF GOD, 8

God corresponds to Godself. That is the basis for Barth's theology and perhaps even the thread that ties it all together. This is why God *is* the subject of God's revelation, why God reveals Godself. God reveals who God is in God's acts towards us in Jesus Christ. Barth writes:

> *God* reveals Himself. He reveals Himself *through Himself.* He reveals *Himself.* If we really want to understand revelation in terms of its subject, i.e., God, then the first thing we have to do is realise that this subject, God, the Revealer, is identical with His act in revelation and also identical with its effect. It is from this fact [...] that we learn we must begin the doctrine of revelation with the doctrine of the Triune God.
>
> — CD I/1, 296

From this, Barth develops the Triunity of God as Revealer, Revelation, and Revealedness. It is because the content of revelation is God revealing Godself through Godself that this is where we must begin. "God's Word is identical with God Himself" (*CD* I/1, 304). To begin anywhere else would be to fall back into mythology or natural theology.

In revelation, we have to do with the Father, Son, and Holy Spirit, the one God in threefold repetition: Revealer, Revelation, and Revealedness. From this basis, Barth works through an excellent discussion (§9) of the Trinity as the "Unity in Trinity" and "Trinity in Unity" and finally "Triunity." Barth prefers this final term over the standard term "Trinity" because it more fully expresses the doctrine.

Following this, Barth discusses the Father, Son, and Holy Spirit in turn as the Creator, Reconciler, and Redeemer. For Barth, Christian theology in all its diversity and complexity is ultimately a critical reflection on the doctrine of God. Dogmatic theology "can first and last, as a whole and in part, say nothing else but that God is" (*CD* II/1, 258). This does not *reduce* all theology to the doctrine of God—as if God is ever apart from God's acts—but it emphasizes the fact that theology always has at its center the *God who acts,* the living God. The two are never separated. There are no abstract acts of God that are not the acts *of God.* Therefore, volume III of Barth's *Dogmatics,* on creation, is really a doctrine of God the Creator. And volume IV, on reconciliation, is indeed the doctrine of God the Reconciler. And if Barth would have written volume V, on redemption, then we would have read there about God the Redeemer. The whole *Church Dogmatics* is indeed occupied with a single subject, God.

For Barth, theology must develop from a center *in God,* and nowhere else. It is, therefore, a science which bases itself entirely upon its subject. This subject never becomes ours to control but as such, remains a free subject, our Lord, the God who reveals Godself. We, therefore, listen to hear what God has to say about Godself in Jesus Christ or we do not hear God at all. God is not discovered in ourselves but in Jesus Christ and Him alone.

Barth's doctrine of revelation can be difficult to comprehend, but it boils down to speaking of God exclusively in terms of Jesus Christ. Why? Because Jesus Christ is God's self-revelation, God revealing Godself. And furthermore, we must speak of God in terms of God's Triunity. Why? Because God reveals Godself in unimpaired unity and distinction; because we are confronted by the Revealer, the event of Revelation, and the effect of Revelation. That is, we have to speak of God as God has spoken of Godself: as Father, Son, and Holy Spirit. This is the threefold Divine "I," God's being in threefold repetition: Unity in Trinity, Trinity in Unity, Triunity.

Barth reminds us that we have to listen and hear God only as God has given Godself to be heard by us, and to speak of God only as God has spoken of Godself. Because who God reveals Godself to be in the being

and acts of Jesus Christ is who God is eternally in Godself. Our God is
the *living* God, and not a dead or mute God. We must listen and speak of
God only where (and in the same manner that) God has spoken of
Godself.

SIGNIFICANCE: Barth revolutionized the way we think about the Trinity
by placing this doctrine at the *beginning* of his *Dogmatics*. Compared to
Schleiermacher's *Christian Faith,* which placed the Trinity in the epilogue
of his system built around the "feeling of absolute dependence," or with
Kant, who saw no practical significance at all for the doctrine of the
Trinity—Barth is radical in reclaiming the vital importance of the Trinity.
By placing the Trinity front and center, not only in *CD* I/1 but on nearly
every page of the *Dogmatics*, Barth has returned theology to the early
Church's emphasis on the Trinity as the *only* way of speaking about God.
The Trinity is arguably *the* doctrine of the early Church, the doctrine
defended and argued the most passionately by great Church fathers such
as Athanasius, Irenaeus, Augustine, Cyril, and Basil. Modern theology has
seen a revolution in Trinitarian theology following Barth's thoroughly
Trinitarian structure.

Furthermore, the positive contribution of Barth's doctrine of revelation is a counter to his rejection of natural theology. In saying No to
natural theology, Barth says Yes to Jesus Christ as the only way in which
we know God. When we look at the person of Jesus Christ, we are seeing
God's very being for us, God's self-revelation in our humanity. Therefore,
if we imagine a God somehow *different* than the God revealed in Jesus
Christ, we must abandon such an image as an idol created by our own
hands. We can only seek God and find the knowledge of God where God
has given Godself to be known and seen by us, in Jesus Christ. This
constant focus on the person of Jesus Christ would single-handedly revo-
lutionize a vast majority of Christian theology today as well as preaching
and pastoral efforts. Barth reminds us that to see Jesus is to see the Father
(John 14:9). Barth's doctrine of revelation is a thorough and faithful
exegesis of Paul's extraordinary remark that Jesus Christ is the "image of
the invisible God" (Col. 1:15).

SIDEBAR: GOD WITHOUT JESUS

Barth's theology challenges us to think of God exclusively in terms of Jesus Christ because in Him alone we have the full revelation of God. In Him, the "fullness of deity" dwells; He is the "image of the invisible God." Any theology which imagines a "God without Jesus," a God formed in our own image and by our own strength, is a theology we must reject.

In an early sermon preached on Matthew 14:22-33 (where Peter steps out on the water to meet Jesus), Barth recognizes a call for our total dependence on the God who is with us in Jesus Christ. Barth writes:

> God without Jesus Christ, God only in our thoughts and feelings or in some home-made portrait such as 'religions' offer, such gods are illusions indeed. Their God is a ghost, a phantom and a delusion, a far-away and unapproachable God. But now He is really with us, as near to us as only the dearest and best friend is near us in an hour of direst distress. [...] Here is Jesus Christ. For Jesus Christ is and means God, but God at the place of my guilt; God with me in my deep misery; God for me and not for Himself. What we really know of Him and whatever help we have

from Him in our sorrow, sin and death, we know and have in Jesus Christ.

— God's Search for Man, 34-5

Theology walks on water with Jesus; it does not build its own boat from humanistic logic. Natural theology is the vessel we often cling to when we are confronted with the miracle of revelation, of Jesus walking on water towards us. Barth's rejection of natural theology is the removal of any theology which rests on *our* comfortable assurances. We are called to step out of the boat, to cease looking for God in our own strength, and to find ourselves upheld and embraced by God in the (humanly) impossible event of knowing God. God makes Godself known to us—that is a miracle. We cannot make this miracle happen, but we must fix our eyes on Jesus Christ, thinking of God exclusively in terms of Him and Him alone; only in this way can we know what God is like.

The only true foundation for theology is the one we cannot build ourselves. We reject any God we imagine exists without Jesus Christ, any God we might come to know *apart* from Him. We reject natural theology and step out onto the water of dependence upon Jesus Christ alone as God's self-revelation in our humanity. God's grace has confronted us in Jesus; we would be fools to cling to the boat of our own intellect, to cling to natural theology.

SIDEBAR: MODALISM

Barth's doctrine of the Trinity is unique for many reasons, but one misunderstanding often brought up is the claim that it is a borderline *modalist* doctrine of the Trinity.

Modalism is the notion that God is one "person" appearing in three modes or forms, that God is not eternally in Godself Father, Son, and Holy Spirit, but merely *appears* to us in this way. Father, Son, and Spirit are thus *masks* God wears. Essentially, modalism claims that God *is not* in Godself who God is in revelation. But as we've seen, Barth's whole theology centers around God being in Godself who God is towards us in Jesus Christ. Accordingly, modalism has no place in his theology, and it is a grave misunderstanding to claim that it does.

This misunderstanding comes from Barth's rejection of a common term traditionally used in statements about the Trinity. Instead of the phrase, "one God in three *persons*," Barth opts for the alternative phrase, "one God in threefold *mode (or way) of being*."

The reason for this terminology is in line with Barth's dedication to speaking of God only in terms of how God has spoken of Godself; and furthermore, it is to forbid our speech about God from becoming *human-centric* speech but *God-centric* by following the logic inherent to God's own Word about Godself. Thus Barth rejects the term "person" because it mistakenly implies that there are three *personalities* in God. Furthermore, the root of the word "person," in both English and German, implies a *mask*. (*Persona,* in Latin, was a term used for actors on a stage, who literally or figuratively wore masks to hide their true identity; it is the root for both person and personen, in English and German, respectively.) In this sense, Barth is hoping to protect the doctrine of the Trinity from the heresy of both tritheism and modalism. Barth writes about this terminology:

> [B]y preference we do not use the term 'person' but rather 'mode (or way) of being,' our intention being to express by this term, not absolutely, but relatively better and more simply and clearly the same thing as is meant by 'person.'

> — CD I/1, 359

Barth intends to retain the biblical meaning of the word "person" with "mode of being," but protects the doctrine of the Trinity from tritheism and modalism by directly refuting this idea of God as three gods, each with independent personalities, or that the Father, Son, and Spirit are merely *masks* God wears. "Person" inadvertently implies personality, and Barth, therefore, opts for "mode of being" as a more precise term.

It is an inexcusably lazy reading of Barth to assume that by using "modes of being" he advocates for modalism. Modalism is a heresy that stands in sharp contrast with Barth's entire theology of revelation. For Barth, God is in Godself who God is towards us in God's acts. For a modalist, the God who appears to us in threefold repetition is *not* who God is in Godself. Modalism cannot say that "God corresponds to Himself" (Jüngel's phrase) or that God is who God is in God's acts. Modalism in practice *denies* revelation because behind Jesus Christ there stands an unknown, monadic divine being. God's threefold distinction as Father, Son, and Holy Spirit, for a modalist, is not how God is in Godself but only how God makes Godself *appear* to us, as a *mask*. Barth rejects this, however, writing:

> Revelation and revealing must be equal to the revealer. Otherwise there is no room for them beside the revealer if this be the one God. The unity of God would render revelation and revealing

impossible. Christ and the Spirit would not just be foreign to and totally unlike the Father, as Arius said in dangerous proximity to a denial of all revelation. They would have no more to do with Him than any other creatures. Only the substantial equality of Christ and the Spirit with the Father is compatible with monotheism.

— CD I/1, 353

We have to say with Barth that God is in Godself who God is towards us; to deny this is to deny revelation. It is not modalism but the desire to speak of God accurately in the same way God has spoken of Godself that necessitates Barth's preference for "mode of being" over the more traditional term "person." In this sense, it is his defense of revelation.

3

THE THREEFOLD WORD OF GOD

SUMMARY: The Word of God addresses the community and the individual *directly* and *indirectly* in what Barth calls the "threefold Word of God." Directly, the Word of God is God's revelation of Godself: Jesus Christ, the Word made flesh. Indirectly, or by mediation, the written Scriptures give witness to revelation and the Church's proclamation witnesses to revelation under the authority and freedom of Holy Scripture. The Church and theology are bound to the Word of God in all three forms because this is how God speaks.

IN BARTH'S OWN WORDS:

The Word of God preached means [...] man's talk about God in which and through which God speaks about Himself. [...]

The Bible is God's Word to the extent that God causes it to be His Word. [...] The statement that the Bible is God's Word is a confession of faith, a statement of the faith which hears God Himself speak through the Biblical word of man. [...]

Revelation does not differ from the person of Jesus Christ nor from the reconciliation accomplished in Him. To say revelation is to say 'The Word became flesh.'

— CD I/1: Word of God proclaimed (95), written (109-10), and revealed (119)

The Word of God is the word of His grace. And if you ask me where we hear this Word of God, I can only point to Himself, who enables us to hear it, and reply with the mighty centre of the Confession, with the second article, that the Word of God's grace in which He meets us is called Jesus Christ, the Son of God and Son of man, true God and true Man, Immanuel, God with us in this One. Christian faith is the meeting with this 'Immanuel', the meeting with Jesus Christ and in Him with the living Word of God. In calling Holy Scripture the Word of God (and we so call it, because it is so); we mean by it Holy Scripture as the witness of the prophets and the apostles to this one Word of God, to Jesus, the man out of Israel, who is God's Christ, our Lord and King in eternity. And in confessing this, in venturing to call the Church's proclamation God's Word, we must be understood to mean the proclamation of Jesus Christ, of Him who is true God and true Man for our good. In Him God meets us.

— Dogmatics in Outline, 17

Secondary quotes:

[Barth] speaks of the Word of God which is preached, of the written Word of God in Holy Scripture, and finally, of the revealed Word of God which, in its fullest form, is Jesus Christ.

— David L. Mueller: Karl Barth, 55

The Bible, therefore, can be said to be the Word of God only in an indirect sense, only because it is creaturely object in conjunction *with* which God speaks to us. [...] We say the *Bible* is the Word of God, because it witnesses to Jesus who *is* the Word of God. So the Bible has material substantive authority, not in itself, not in its own words on the page, not in the facts, events, ideas, images, or propositions recorded therein. The material authority of the Bible is identical with Jesus Christ, the living Word of God who speaks here and now in 'a divine act of majesty.'

— ARNOLD B. COME: AN INTRODUCTION TO BARTH'S
DOGMATICS FOR PREACHERS, 172

GOD SPEAKS

The Word of God is threefold. It is God in revelation, God speaking in Holy Scripture, and God speaking in Church proclamation. In the previous chapter we discussed the nature of revelation (God reveals God only through Godself, i.e., God's Triunity), and in this chapter, we now ask how it is we hear revelation. How do we come to know Revelation and thus speak of what only God can know and what only God can speak of?

For this Barth develops the creative and practical doctrine of the threefold Word of God. This includes God's *direct* Word in the person of Jesus Christ, God's self-revelation. But there is also God's *indirect*—or mediated—Word witnessed to in the Scriptures and the Church's proclamation (preaching).

The problem at the heart of this is how human words can become God's Word about Godself? How can Revelation reach us, if all we have available is the witness of Scripture and the proclamation of the Church? The simple answer is: *God speaks.* God wills to speak in this way, in and through the witness of the human words of Scripture and Church proclamation.

These are essentially pointers, a "sign," attesting to God's revelation of Godself, but as such, they are mediums through which God speaks about Godself. This is why we have called them mediated or indirect forms of the Word of God. Yet they are no less the Word of God. This is not because they are in themselves special words (apart from grace), but because God has spoken and still speaks and will continue speaking through them because God has revealed Godself in Jesus Christ. These witnesses speak of Him. They are therefore not merely human words anymore but become God's Word about Godself, God's own self-witness through these human witnesses.

Barth writes, "The Bible is God's Word so far as God lets it be His Word, so far as God speaks through it" (*CD* I/1, 123). And elsewhere, emphasizing the Spirit's role in causing the Scriptures to "become" God's Word, Barth writes, "Scripture is holy and the Word of God, because by the Holy Spirit it became and will become to the Church a witness to divine revelation" (*CD* I/2, 457). This indicates a *dynamic* understanding of the Bible so that in itself it is only God's Word as God speaks in and through it. God's word remains free and is not transformed into an object of human control, even in the witness of Scripture.

Barth's chapters on "The Witness" and "The Community" in *Evangelical Theology* helpfully summarize Scripture and Church proclamation as the primary and secondary *witnesses* to revelation. We have then The Word, which is direct revelation (Jesus Christ), The Witness, which is Scripture, and The Community, which is Church proclamation. The witness of the Church is bound to the witness of Scripture, just as the witness of Scripture is bound to revelation. The Scriptures are the primary and the proclamation of the Church the secondary witnesses to revelation. This is the *distinction* between the threefold Word of God, which does not at once mean a *division*. There are not three words of God but only the one Word of God, Jesus Christ, and this includes God's indirect speech about Godself through the Holy Spirit in Scripture and in the Church.

Barth stresses that *primarily* God's Word is the person of Jesus Christ, but at once he recognizes we cannot know direct revelation apart from the witnesses of Scripture and preaching. Both forms of witness, by the Holy Spirit, *become* God's Word as God speaks through them, acting as God's own witness in and through these human mediums. Theology is therefore bound to the Word of God in all three forms.

We'll now discuss each of these forms of God's Word in turn.

THE WRITTEN WORD OF GOD

By speaking of Scripture as the *witness* to the Word of God, Barth makes an important distinction often lacking in the way many individuals approach the Bible. The Scriptures cannot be directly equated with revelation itself; they bear *witness* to revelation, but they are not in and of themselves revelation apart from the miracle of grace. There are two anchoring thoughts behind this concept. The first is that Scripture is a witness to revelation and not revelation itself; and the second is that Scripture *becomes* God's Word as God speaks through it, as the Holy Spirit bears witness to Jesus Christ in and through its human words. The first emphasizes the *humanity* of the Bible, and the second highlights God's will to speak in and through that humanity.

With this Barth warns against the dual error of Docetism and Ebionitism. The former is the heresy that Jesus Christ was not human but only divine, and the latter is the heresy that Jesus Christ was only human and not divine. An analogy can be drawn between these heresies and our understanding of the Bible. That much becomes clear in Barth's ability to stand between both conservative and liberal readings of the Bible. Barth thinks that conservatives often fall into the error of Docetism, of a *divine* Bible with minimal humanity; while liberals often fall into the error of Ebionitism, of a *human* Bible with minimal divinity. Barth's doctrine of Holy Scripture attempts to stand between both errors. Thus Barth rejects the notion of Biblical inerrancy, which most conservatives affirm, but he at once does not fall into the liberal error of assuming to have a superior platform from which he might judge where the Bible is in error (such as Bultmann's form-criticism). So while Barth would resist ever saying unequivocally that the Bible is without error (it has the "vulnerability" or "capacity for error," he says), Barth at once would refuse to point to any such error.

For Barth, reading the Scripture involves studying its earthly-historical context; we best understand it as both human words about God written within their historical and cultural limitations, and as God's Word miraculously spoken in these fallible human words. Barth goes so far as to call an "unhistorical" reading of the Bible an "unbiblical" reading (*CD* I/2, 466-7). Why? Because this is how the Bible itself insists that we read it, historically.

Barth's ultimate goal in approaching the Scripture is to let God's Word truly be *God's* Word. This allows Barth to make several, self-admittedly, circular reasons for the authority of the Bible. But at the heart of this is Barth's dedication to letting the Word speak.

Thomas F. Torrance calls this willingness to *listen* to the Word of Scripture the "secret of Barth's hermeneutic," adding:

Biblical exegesis takes place therefore in a strenuous disciplined attempt to lay ourselves open to hear the Word of God speaking to us, to read what the Word intends or denotes and to refrain from interrupting it or confusing it with our own speaking, for in faithful exegesis we have to let ourselves be told what we cannot tell ourselves.

— KARL BARTH, 22

Learning to listen and hear God in Scripture begins with faith in God's ability to speak through the fallible human witness of the Bible. Barth writes:

The statement that the Bible is God's Word is a confession of faith, a statement of the faith which hears God Himself speak through the Biblical word of man. [...] [This confession is] that the Bible is God's Word, the little word 'is' refers to its being in this becoming.

— CD I/1, 110

The Bible is God's Word to the extent that God causes it to be His Word.

— CD I/1, 109

That God speaks in the Bible is a *confession* of the Church; that the Scriptures *become* God's Word is a reality acknowledge only by faith. It is a miracle that we hear God's Word in the human words of the Bible, but it is a miracle we must confess. We cannot confirm this claim, nor should we seek to support it. As God's Word it is *God's* Word and not *our* words about God, even if it is witnessed to in human words. Thus God has the controlling authority over God's Word, taking the problem of our desire for assurance and certainty out of our hands. In the event of faith, we hear God's speech about Godself in and through the human witness of Scripture, and therefore Scripture *becomes* God's Word by the Holy Spirit. This is the *written* Word.

THE REVEALED WORD OF GOD

What is "direct" revelation? Simply, Jesus Christ: His person and the work of reconciliation accomplished in Him. Barth writes, "Revelation in fact does not differ from the person of Jesus Christ nor from the reconciliation accomplished in Him. To say revelation is to say 'The Word became flesh'" (*CD* I/1, 119). Almost exclusively, whenever Barth talks about revelation he means the person and work of Jesus Christ who is the content of God's self-revelation. This direct form of revelation was the subject of our previous chapter: God's self-revelation and self-interpretation, the threefold "I" of Father, Son, and Holy Spirit. This is the *revealed* Word.

THE PROCLAIMED WORD OF GOD

The Church proclaims the Word of God. This is the final form of the threefold Word of God. Here Barth shows his concern with Christian preaching. For Barth, a primary task of dogmatics is to assist in the task of preaching. His *Dogmatics* was not meant to be a scholarly resource exclusively—although this is the way it has been understood the most. It is, however, also a tremendous resource for preaching. Barth argued that the task of dogmatics stands in between that of exposition (biblical theology) and application (practical theology). Dogmatics is to maintain a close relationship with both. The task of dogmatics is therefore never merely pure speculation or a purely academic endeavor without first having a basis in the life of the Church. G. W. Bromiley summarized this emphasis, writing, "The problem of preaching is the problem of dogmatics; the problem of dogmatics is the problem of preaching" (*Introduction to the Theology of Karl Barth*, 46).

Preaching can never escape the task of theology, nor can the task of theology avoid that of preaching. They belong together. A good example of this can be seen in Barth's own life. Late in life, Barth regularly preached to Basel prisoners. These sermons are collected in the books *Deliverance to the Captives* and *Call for God*, and they contain some of Barth's most moving, pastoral remarks. Theology is not an abstract science but always strives to assist in the proclamation of the gospel.

"The Word of God preached means [...] man's talk about God in which and through which God speaks about Himself" (*CD* I/1, 95). Preaching is a form of the threefold Word of God, in which God speaks about Godself in human words. It is worth briefly noting here that Barth preferred the term *proclamation* instead of preaching. This was to give a broader scope for the Church's proclamation, namely, to include its sacraments. Barth never completed a full exposition of the sacraments— though it was planned for *CD* IV, and he did produce a small part-volume on baptism (IV/4) in which his understanding of the "sacraments" changed drastically. (Compare *CD* I/2 and *CD* IV/4.) But it is worth noting that Barth originally gave place for the sacraments to have a part of God's Word in Church proclamation. However, the emphasis often falls on preaching.

Preaching becomes God's Word by the Holy Spirit speaking in and through its feeble human witness. Since preaching only has the word of Scripture as its basis and authority, it is called a *secondary* form of witness. The Church is bound to the authority and freedom of the Scriptures, and therefore its proclamation stands under the Word of God in the Bible.

Barth maintains the distinction between the witness and the object witnessed to. However, he rightly understood that since God alone reveals Godself, God must speak in and through these witnesses, turning them into God's own self-witness. Therefore, the Church's proclamation *becomes* God's Word by the Holy Spirit. This is the *proclaimed* Word.

THE UNITY OF THE THREEFOLD WORD OF GOD

Barth stresses the unity of the threefold Word of God. We have already noted that there is an order to the threefold Word of God. First, there is direct revelation, Jesus Christ. Second, there is the witness of the prophets and apostles in Holy Scripture. Third, there is the Church's proclamation under the authority and freedom of Scripture. These are not three separate words about God but God's Word in threefold form. The unity of God's Word in all three forms depends on understanding the mutual relations between each. Barth describes this relationship:

> The Revealed Word of God we know only from the Scripture adopted by Church proclamation or the proclamation of the Church based on Scripture.

The written Word of God we know only through the revelation which fulfills proclamation or through the proclamation fulfilled by revelation.

The preached Word of God we know only through the revelation attested in Scripture or the Scripture which attests revelation.

— CD I/1, 121

Barth notes that this is the only true analogy possible for the Triunity of God since this is God's Word, God speaking about Godself, in three-fold repetition and unimpaired unity. Though ultimately we cannot place too much emphasis on such an analogy, because God is without equal and therefore cannot become the object of an analogy. Therefore, this only works as an analogy from the Trinity *to* the threefold Word of God and not the reverse. Noting this analogy, however, helps us see the unity and distinction of the threefold Word of God as it is revealed, written, and proclaimed.

SIGNIFICANCE: Barth's doctrine of the threefold Word of God is a helpful way to understand how we do theology and how we are to know God's self-revelation. It answers the question of how we may come to participate in God's knowledge of Godself since the event of revelation is exclusively Jesus Christ. Therefore, God bears witness to Godself in and through the human witnesses of Scripture and preaching. Through the Holy Spirit, we encounter God's self-revelation and self-interpretation in reading the scriptural witness and hearing the Church's proclamation. God's truth about Godself is mediated in this personal encounter. We participate by grace in God's knowledge of Godself, as God speaks to us in this threefold form. It is by grace that God speaks to us today in this way, and Barth reminds us to *listen* to the Word of God faithfully and attentively where God has spoken it.

SIDEBAR: BIBLICAL INERRANCY

It may be helpful to engage Barth with the contemporary question of Biblical inerrancy. Biblical inerrancy is essentially the idea that the Scriptures are *without error* in and of themselves. The "Chicago Statement on Biblical Inerrancy" from 1978 puts it like this: the Protestant Bible is "without error or fault in all its teaching." This concept is sometimes joined with Biblical *infallibility*, but not everyone equates inerrancy with infallibility.

How does Barth's doctrine of Scripture fit in with this contemporary discussion? Many Evangelical pastors and theologians have rejected Barth as a dangerous theologian because of his rejection of inerrancy, while others have hailed his approach as a helpful way forward beyond the fundamentalism imbedded in Biblical inerrancy.

Barth argues that the Scriptures *are* vulnerable to error, they contain a "capacity for error" since they are *human* words. He stresses the humanity of the Scripture but at once its authority as God's Word. Furthermore, while there remains the *possibility* of error in the Bible, Barth refuses to point out any such error: "Instead of talking about the 'errors' of the Biblical authors in this sphere, if we want to go to the heart of things it is better to speak only about their 'capacity for errors'" (*CD* I/2, 508).

Barth makes the distinction between the Word of God and the human words of the Bible: "Scripture does indeed bear witness to revelation, but it is not revelation itself" (*Göttingen Dogmatics* vol. 1, 202). He does not deny that Scripture is God's Word and therefore authoritative, but instead makes a careful distinction between what the Bible is and what it isn't. The Scriptures contain human words, written as a witness to God's self-revelation. Barth calls it a *miracle* that in these human words we hear God's Word, writing, "To say 'the Word of God' is to say the miracle of God" (*CD* I/2, 528). Thus, the Bible is not in itself infallible except by grace. Because God speaks, we hear God, not because the text itself is perfect. It is *suitable,* but not necessarily flawless.

Recognizing this forces us to rely upon the grace of God, and not upon the presupposed "perfection" of a book. The problem with misunderstanding this distinction is that we inevitably make the Bible "an instrument separated from the free grace of God and put into the hands of man" (*CD* I/2, 523). Inerrancy fails to understand the miracle of the Scriptures as God's Word by mistaking them for direct revelation, and thus, in turn, it makes the Bible an independent source of revelation apart from grace, i.e., apart from God. Plainly, *an inerrant Bible is a Bible that does not need God.*

That is one of Barth's primary concerns. We cannot mistake Scripture with *direct* revelation. The Scriptures bear witness to revelation, but they are not in themselves directly identified with revelation. God's Word is not bound; it remains free. Barth colorfully says that when we mistakenly identify the Scriptures with direct revelation, we turn the Bible into a "paper pope." Barth writes:

> The texts bear *witness,* and *the texts* are the witness that we are to perceive. [...] The Bible is not the same as revelation. [...] For this reason, precisely on a theological view, the 17th-century doctrine of verbal inspiration, the idea that the Biblical authors did not think and write on their own but simply took down heavenly dictation, is so deplorable. This view changes revelation into direct revelation. It thus sets it aside. It does not just put Scripture in the pope's place but makes it a pope, a paper pope, from which we are to get oracles as we get shoes from the shoemaker.
>
> — Göttingen Dogmatics Vol. 1, 216-7

This is the result of "grounding the Bible on itself, apart from the mystery of Christ and the Holy Ghost" (*CD* I/2, 525).

Barth offers the Pool of Bethesda as an analogy for the correct way we should understand the miracle of God's Word in Holy Scripture:

> A genuine, fallible human word is at this centre the Word of God: not in virtue of its own superiority, of its replacement by a Word of God veiled as the word of man, still less of any kind of miraculous transformation, but, of course, in virtue of the privilege that here and now it is taken and used by God Himself, like the water in the Pool of Bethesda.
>
> — CD I/2, 530

It is a grievous mistake to overlook the humanity of the Bible. We do not find divine oracles contained in its pages, but human words within a specific historical and cultural situation. God miraculously uses these human words to speak *the* Word, but in and of themselves and apart from the miracle of grace, these human words are fallible, limited, and vulnerable words. That is important to stress for understanding Barth's doctrine of Scripture. As we've noted, Barth stands between the dual errors of Docetism and Ebionitism, of over-emphasizing either the humanity or the divinity of the Bible. Inerrancy tends to make the Bible into a divine oracle of systematic truths, but this falls into the error of Docetism and therefore neglects the humanity of the Biblical witness. We must emphasize *both* the humanity of the Bible and the divine miracle of God's speaking in and through these human words.

For an insightful example of how Barth applies his understanding of the Scripture as witness, we'll examine how he deals with the Bible's witness to creation in the form of "saga" or "story." Barth writes:

> The Biblical witnesses speak as men and not as angels or gods. Thus we have to reckon on their part with all kinds of human factors, with their individual and general capacities of perception and expression, with their personal views and style, as determined by age and environment, and of course with the limitations and deficiencies of these conditioning factors [...]. The Biblical

creation-histories are not heaven-sent declarations of truth itself dropped from the sky but human attestations of the revelation which has taken place in the creaturely sphere. It is in this way, and only in this way, that they declare truth. They do this in relation to what God has given to certain men to apprehend concerning Himself, and they do it through the imagination and lips and writings of these men who in themselves are as fallible as others. They are not, then, an adequate but a very inadequate medium. In respect of their content and credibility, they live wholly by their object, i.e., by the self-witness of the Holy Spirit to whom alone they owe their origin and power. This is the determination and limitation which we must not overlook in our appreciation and interpretation of them. Their relationship to their object is the very unequal one of a heavenly treasure to earthly vessels to which it has been entrusted for preservation and impartation. But this relationship is their mystery and miracle. It is in this relationship, and only in this relation, that they are inspired and speak the Word of God. [...]

If and because the task of interpretation is to bring to light the reality of the historical self-revelation of God to which they bear witness, the human side of their witness as such must not be overlooked or expunged, but introduced even in its humanity and therefore its frailty and problematic character, although with no shame that it has so concrete a form; with no desire, in the face of this concrete form, to be better informed by the imported presuppositions of the interpreter; with no haste to amend or improve it, or to cover its indisputable nakedness, or to abandon it where its human limitation seems too palpable and disturbing to the expositor. How do we know whether the self-witness of its object is not loudest and most important precisely where its historical and linguistic determination, the fallibility of the writers and the limitation and deficiency of their imagination, seem to strike us most forcibly? A thoughtful interpretation will be all the more careful and reverent with the Biblical witness when its humanity is most clearly recognised: not for its own sake; not out of any magical respect for the letter, which as such is a letter like others; but out of respect for the object which has not been ashamed to raise up these human witnesses with their limitations and to make use of this letter, and which we can know, if at all, only through this witness, and through the letter of this witness.

— CD III/1, 93-4

We could recognize four points from this passage:

1. The Scriptures are a *human* witness to God's self-revelation. As such they are *God's Word* in and through *human* words. These human words do not become divine, heavenly gifted words—and thus perfect words in the language of angels!—but these human words are God's Word *because* God has chosen these words to witness to God's Word.

2. Recognizing the humanity of the Scriptures does not destroy its *authority*, but instead establishes its authority as it rests not on *itself* but on the *object* of its witness, on the Word of God.

3. The humanity of the Scriptures cannot be erased by attempting to "correct" their human-ness. Barth warns that perhaps it is precisely in the *humanity* of the Bible that the witness of God's Word is to be heard most clearly. The humanity of the Bible is not an obstacle to be overcome, but a form of grace as God makes Godself known through its witness.

4. In this sense, the Scriptures are both the human witness to God's Word and God's Word itself in human witness. God has decided to use these human words as God's own Word, to speak infallible Word of God in the form of a fallible human witness. It is in this sense that the Scriptures *become* God's Word out of the witness of human words because God determines these words as God's own witness.

Where does this leave us with Biblical inerrancy? While Barth passed away before the Chicago Statement on inerrancy, he would have likely reacted negatively towards it for three major reasons. First, inerrancy attempts to make the humanity of the Bible a kind of angelic/divine humanity, thus stripping the Scripture of its capacity for error. Second, inerrancy confuses the witness to the truth with the object witnessed, the form with the content. But God's Word is not controlled by or subject to its human witness; its human witness is controlled by and subjected to God's Word.

Third, and most importantly, for Barth Biblical inerrancy is problematic because it attempts to build up a foundation which is *different* from the only true foundation: Jesus Christ. It confuses divine revelation with the witness of Scripture to divine revelation.

Barth warns that we must retain an awareness of the *mystery* of God's Word in Holy Scripture:

> We should not try to master the text. The Bible will become more and more mysterious to real exegetes. They will see all the depths and distances. They will constantly run up against the mystery before which theology is trying to drain the ocean with a spoon. The true exegete will face the text like an astonished child in a wonderful garden, not like an advocate of God who has seen all his files.
>
> — HOMILETICS, 128

Biblical inerrancy removes the mystery of the Scriptures by attempting to master them in identifying their content with the truth; but that truth is not theirs to own or master, it is always *God's* truth standing above human words. God gives us self-revelation in the Scriptures, but God does not give Godself *up*. God remains free in God's revelation against our systematic attempt of mastering or containing the Word.

Biblical inerrancy ultimately ignores the need for *faith in God*. If the Scriptures are without error and contain objective truths sent from heaven, then the need for us to have faith in a God who makes Godself known even through fallible human witnesses is deemed unnecessary. Accepting that the Scriptures contain a capacity for error does not deny their authority. In fact, this affirms more forcefully the authority of Scripture *on God's strength* and not on our own. The Bible is not authoritative in and of itself, but only in faith, as God uses human words to speak God's Word by grace. This faith is not in a book written by human beings, but in the God who has determined to speak in and through these human words. We do not believe in a book, we believe in Jesus Christ, proclaimed in Holy Scripture.

Thomas F. Torrance succinctly summarizes Barth's understanding of the Scriptures in contrast with Biblical inerrancy. Torrance writes:

The Word of God comes to us in the Bible through the speech of sinful, fallible men to whom God has spoken and who bear witness to his speaking. We do not have here a direct speaking of God from heaven, but a speaking through a transient and imperfect human medium. No doubt the human word we hear in the Scriptures is not always appropriate or adequate to the Word which its authors have heard and to which they bear testimony, but nevertheless it is human word which God has freely chosen and decided to use as the form in which he speaks his Word to us. It is that objective side of the Scripture, the object of its testimony, that gives the Scripture its fundamental character as holy and inspired Word. [...]

It is important, then, to recognise that in the Bible there is this 'wall' between us and divine Revelation, namely, the man-conditioned and time-conditioned character of the witness. If we deny or ignore it, then we turn the Bible into an organ of direct and immediate oracular communication, and, in point of fact, [we] deny Revelation itself, that is, deny God himself in his Revelation whom we hear and know only in decisive encounter and to whom we respond in faith and obedience.

— KARL BARTH: AN INTRODUCTION TO HIS EARLY
THEOLOGY 1910-1931, 120-1

At the end of the day, Barth's doctrine of the threefold Word of God inspires deeper *confidence* in the Scriptures; not because they are special in themselves, but because God wills to and does speak through its imperfect witness. While Barth maintains the capacity for error included in the humanity of the scriptural witness, this does not negate God's freedom to speak in and through its witness. Instead, Barth removes any *human* confidence we might have in the Bible, replacing it with singular confidence in God's ability to *speak* through this human witness in all its weakness. That *God speaks* in Scripture places our trust not in the excellence of its witness, but in the excellence of Him to whom it bears witness.

A final, cautionary note should be made in closing. Barth's doctrine of Holy Scripture is one of his most controversial proposals, in the sense that many will outright reject Barth (likely before ever reading him) because of it. That is especially true for American Evangelicals who put so much weight on the issue of Biblical inerrancy. But my recommendation for those who might be on the fence about Barth's doctrine of Scripture is simply to read it first for yourself before forming rash judgments. There are many good reasons *why* Barth develops this doctrine the way he does. It is not to subvert the authority of the scriptures or to make truth relative to please "itching" ears. Barth argues at great length for the authority of the Scriptures in the Church, and he certainly does not want to relativize it or water that authority down. This is a common complaint against those who question Biblical inerrancy, but I recommend reading Barth first before mindlessly repeating these unfounded complaints.

Read *CD* I/2 chapter III on Holy Scripture, §19 especially but also §20-21 (pages 457-740). If you still find Barth's doctrine unacceptable, at least you will do so with a clear understanding of what Barth says. You are free (and encouraged) to disagree with Barth on many things, but you are not free to disagree with him or reject him outright *before* reading him for yourself.

SERMON: THEY BEAR WITNESS TO ME

The Bible bears witness to Jesus Christ; He is its fundamental message. In a sermon, Barth declared:

> This is Jesus. It is the message of every story in the New Testament as well as the Old. *'They bear witness of me'* applies to all the Scriptures. The whole Bible has no other content, in the last analysis, than to testify of Him who is coming from above. Its only purpose is to spell and speak out the name JESUS, in order to tell us, in and with His name, of GOD. But the God of the Bible is not the puny little godlet which men fashion for themselves with their concepts. No; He is the true and real God, the God who IS God, the God who doeth wondrous things.
>
> — GOD'S SEARCH FOR MAN, 28

While the Bible tells us many things, the central element is its witness to Jesus Christ; its testimony about His coming, about His life, death, and resurrection, and about His coming again in glory.

"You search the Scriptures because you think that in them you have eternal life; and it is they that testify on my behalf" (John 5:39, NRSV). It is easy for us to fall into the same trap and search the Scriptures for life while we miss the One who *is* life. Barth's doctrine of the threefold Word of God helps us keep this careful distinction in place.

It would be a mistake to identify the Word of God with a book. It would also be a mistake not to listen and hear the Word of God in and through that book. These two distinctions are the pillars which hold up the Bible as the witness to God's Word. It is not God's Word in itself, but God speaks through it, and it becomes God's Word by grace.

We aren't splitting hairs here for the sake of confusion. The purpose of this distinction is to maintain the central place Jesus Christ has for the whole witness of the Bible. The Scriptures bear witness to Christ, to the living God who speaks today still in and through the testimony of Scripture. This book is worth our attention not because it is inherently special, but because *God* has spoken about Godself, about Jesus Christ, in and through its pages. It is this Word we must carefully listen for on every page.

4

NO HIDDEN GOD BEHIND THE BACK OF JESUS CHRIST

SUMMARY: There is no hidden God behind the back of Jesus Christ for us to fear; God reveals Godself unreservedly in Christ. Divine revelation, therefore, forbids theological speculation about God. God remains mysterious still in revelation because the truth of God's self-disclosure is *mediated* truth. God is hidden precisely *because* God is revealed. The hiddenness of God moves theology away from thinking with a center in human beings to a center in God's self-revelation. There is no hidden God behind the revealed God, but the revealed God *is* God in hiddenness.

IN BARTH'S OWN WORDS:

In the revelation of God, there is no hidden God, no *Deus absconditus,* at the back of His revelation, with whose existence and activity we have also occasionally to reckon beyond His Word and His Spirit, and whom we have also to fear and honour behind His revelation. [...] God is God and therefore mystery. But in this very mystery He encounters and gives Himself to man without reservation, without our having to wait for another.

— CD II/1, 210-11

There is no greater depth in God's being and work than that [which is] revealed in these happenings and under this name [Jesus Christ]. For in these happenings and under this name He has revealed Himself.

— CD II/2, 54

That Jesus is the one Word of God means first that He is the total and complete declaration of God concerning Himself and the men whom He addresses in His Word. God does satisfaction both to Himself and us in what He says in and with the existence of Jesus Christ. What He is for us and wills of us, but also what we are for Him and are ordained to be and will and do in this relationship is exhaustively, unreservedly and totally revealed to us in Jesus Christ as the one Word of God.

— CD IV/3.1, 99

SECONDARY QUOTES:

Nothing essential of God's identity ever needs to be sought elsewhere, Barth argued, than in Jesus Christ, God's definitive, final, and binding act of self-revelation. There is no God apart from, beyond, or behind God as God is in Jesus Christ. In Jesus Christ, God's being is present in its unity and entirety. There is no hidden God beyond the revealed God. The hidden God and the revealed God are essentially one and the same. The hiddenness of God is given in and with God's self-revelation, and God's self-revelation does not exclude but includes God's hiddenness. As revealed in trinitarian self-disclosure, God's identity in and with Jesus Christ is ineffaceably mysterious—concealed in the midst of disclosure and disclosed in the midst of concealment.

— GEORGE HUNSINGER: HOW TO READ KARL BARTH, 37

For Barth, God is not the *Deus absconditus;* God is not veiled. For Barth, God is revealed once and for all, definitively, in Christ Jesus.

— RUSTIN E. BRIAN: COVERING UP LUTHER, 108

THE "HIDDENNESS" OF GOD VS. THE HIDDEN GOD

There is a careful distinction Barth makes when he discusses the hiddenness of God in contrast with the hidden God behind revelation. On the one hand, Barth rejects the notion that there is a hidden God behind the back of Jesus Christ, a God we must reckon with who is *different* from Jesus Christ. But on the other hand, Barth affirms God's hiddenness as that which is *included* in God's self-revelation. For Barth, the hidden God and the revealed God are the same. The hiddenness of God, rather than opening the door for abstract speculation about an unknown deity, places a *limit* on our knowledge of God. The God revealed in Jesus Christ is not revealed only partially. God has fully disclosed Godself in Him. The hiddenness of God places a limit on our knowledge of God's revelation by retaining the mystery of God even in self-revelation.

Barth writes to this distinction as early as in his *Göttingen Dogmatics*:

> God's hiddenness, his incomprehensibility, is his hiddenness not alongside or behind revelation but in it. [...] The revealed God and the hidden God are one and the same, and he is the total God, the Lord Sabaoth, beside whom there is no other.
>
> — GÖTTINGEN DOGMATICS VOL. 1, 93

There is no hidden God behind the back of Jesus Christ. Which simply means that if we want to know what God is like, what God *does* and who God *is*, then we look exclusively upon the person and work of Jesus Christ. God is like *this*, and *this* is what God is like. God looks like Jesus, and any attempt to define God apart from Jesus Christ, to discover a God hidden behind the back of Him, is an enterprise we must reject.

This rejection of the hidden God and the careful definition of the hiddenness of God is an essential aspect of Barth's theology. While it is rarely found to be as vital as I am considering it here, I think this is one of the most *pastorally* helpful aspects of Barth's theology. Furthermore, stressing this aspect of Barth's thought emphasizes the central place divine revelation holds for Barth. In this chapter, we'll continue to describe more in detail the hiddenness of God, what it means and why it must be said, in contrast with the idea of a God hidden *behind* revelation. Following this, we will explore its implications with a practical example. We'll show how one of the most common questions posed against God is fundamentally a *speculative* question which inquires about a hidden, hypothetical God rather than the God revealed in Jesus Christ.

The hiddenness of God in Barth's theology

For Barth, the subject and the object of our knowledge of God is God. God is at once the Known and the Knower: the Revealer, the Revelation, and the Revealedness. God knows Godself. Both the means and the end of our knowledge of God is God and not ourselves. We discussed this in chapter two. Remembering this distinction helps us better understand the *mystery*, the hiddenness, of God even in God's self-revelation. We are not talking about an unknown, unpredictable God when we talk about God's hiddenness, but about an uncontrollable or "un-objectifiable" *known*; the living, self-revealing God.

Truth about God is always *mediated* truth. This means that while God makes Godself known to us in Jesus Christ, our knowledge of God is never knowledge *given over* to us as the object of our control. God remains free in Godself and therefore hidden because God has made God known through God. God's revealed Word about Godself remains inapprehensible *because* it is *God's* Word which never becomes *our* word.

Our knowledge of God is, therefore, knowledge by faith because it is through participating in God's knowledge of Godself that we know God at all. It is *mediated* knowledge. In God's revelation we are up against God's definitive Word, not a partial word or a partial revelation, but the total Word of God. And yet this Word is not *immediate* to us or under our control, even if it is at once unveiled unreservedly. God remains a mystery because God remains outside of our grasp and beyond our control. God is free. Knowledge of God does not become *ownership* of God. That we participate in God's knowledge of Godself is an act of grace, a pure gift, through faith. If we know God at all, it is because this is God's work and not our own. As Barth writes, God is "the One who remains [a] mystery to us *because* He Himself has made Himself so clear and certain to us" (*CD* II/1, 43; emphasis mine).

We have no clarity or certainty about God which is not at once God's own clarity and certainty about Godself. It is given to us in Jesus Christ as we share in *His* clarity and certainty, and therefore only in a *secondary* sense. In ourselves, we are often uncertain and confused. Only in Him do we know God, but always by *indirect* participation. Ultimately, Barth's concept of the "hiddenness" of God stresses that in the knowledge of God *we do not begin with ourselves*.

"In Him we have a part in the first and final truth that God is not hidden but revealed to Himself" (*CD* II/1, 154). And the stunning reality is, "Jesus Christ Himself sees to it that in Him and by Him we are not outside but inside" (*CD* II/1, 156). We participate in Christ's knowledge of God, in the full unveiling of God, as a work of the Holy Spirit awakening faith in us. Because this is a knowledge graced to us, gifted to us in Jesus Christ, it is beyond our control and therefore remains a mystery to us. That is how Barth can speak of an absolute certainty in God's self-revelation, that we do not have the unknown, hidden God confronting us but the revealed God; and yet can say at once that God remains hidden precisely *because* God has revealed Godself. The bottom line is how Barth distinguishes between God's knowledge of Godself and our participation in that knowledge by faith, thus excluding the possibility of any knowledge of God centered on ourselves.

The hiddenness of God is thus the limitation of our knowledge of God, the destruction of all our attempts to speculate about what God is like apart from self-revelation. God refuses to give Godself over to be the object of our control.

Barth writes:

The assertion of God's hiddenness tells us that God does not belong to the objects which we can always subjugate to the process of our viewing, conceiving and expressing and therefore our spiritual oversight and control. In contrast to that of all other objects, His nature is not one which in this sense lies in the sphere of our power. God is inapprehensible.

— CD II/1, 187

REMOVING SPECULATION FROM THEOLOGY

Barth's theological emphasis on divine revelation removes all grounds for a *speculative* theology. A speculative theology attempts to go behind revelation, to think unbounded to the person of Jesus Christ and to imagine what God might be like *without* exclusively considering who God has revealed Godself to be in Him. Speculative theology ultimately creates a God *different* from the God revealed in Jesus Christ, an idol fashioned after our own image.

One of the best examples of how quickly we can fall into a speculative theology is when we consider the question of God and human suffering. How many times have you heard the abstract question, "If God is good and all-powerful, why is there suffering in the world?" The issue with this question isn't that the problem of suffering is an unimportant theological problem, but that this question is not fundamentally a *theological* question at all (in the Christian sense of the word). This is a *speculative* question, a question more likely to be found in classic philosophy textbooks than in the Bible—which is precisely where the question originates. The earliest records often cite the Greek philosopher Epicurus for posing this question; it is fundamentally speculative and therefore untheological.

Barth reminds us that if we are to speak of God, we must speak exclusively in terms of God's self-revelation, i.e., in terms of Jesus Christ. This speculative question has nothing whatsoever to do with the person of Jesus Christ. Instead, in the light of revelation, we come to see there is a better way to ask the question of suffering. Two notable theologians indebted to Barth's theology—Jürgen Moltmann and Eberhard Jüngel—have written extensively on how to form a truly *Christian* response to suffering by first asking truly Christian questions. (See Moltmann's *The Crucified God* and Jüngel's *God as the Mystery of the World* for more.)

Instead of speculating about an abstract God, if we want to answer the problem of evil in a Christian way we can only do so by speaking exclusively in terms of Jesus Christ. This means asking concretely where Jesus Christ is in our suffering, and therefore arriving at concrete theological answers, the culmination of which finds its source in the crucifixion. Instead of thinking about an abstract philosophical deity far removed from our suffering, Christian theology must ask theological questions in concrete relation to Jesus Christ who is God with us, God suffering in our humanity, the crucified God.

Christian theology far too often treats itself like a free, speculative philosophy by thinking from a center in human beings rather than exclusively in terms of Jesus Christ. The question of God and suffering is just one example of the speculative tendency in a theology which fails to speak of God in this way. This tendency rests on the idea of a hidden God behind the back of Jesus Christ and ultimately originates from mistrust in divine revelation. In stating that there is no God hidden behind the back of divine revelation, Barth excludes the possibility of speculating about who God is and what God does. For Barth, God looks like Jesus Christ. Period.

On being afraid of God

Barth makes an important clarification about this. The hiddenness of God *does*, in fact, permit us to say that God is *greater* than all that we can say about God. God's love, grace, and patience are greater realities than all the words in all of the languages of all time with which we could attempt to describe God. God is *greater* than our best thoughts. However, what the hiddenness of God *does not do* is allow us to say that God is *different* from what we learn by exclusively looking to Jesus Christ. God has revealed *Godself,* not a word *about* Godself or only some of Godself but indeed God's essential being. We do not have to cope with the possibility of a different God hidden behind the back of Jesus Christ. We must confess that God will ultimately be *greater* than anything we can learn about in our limited humanity, but the hiddenness of God excludes the possibility of God being *different* from self-revelation.

This highlights the fact that God may be *formally* greater than what we know from revelation, but God cannot—because God has in freedom is bound to Jesus Christ—be *materially* different from revelation. This is the critical difference between the notion of a hidden God behind the back of Jesus Christ and of the revealed God in hiddenness.

Barth makes this clarification in regards to God's omnipotence:

We are no longer free but forbidden to reckon on an essentially *different* omnipotence from that which God has manifested in His actual choice and action, as if God could exercise a different choice and action and capacity from what He has done. We can count on a *greater* omnipotence, but not on a *different* one. We can reckon with the freedom with which God willed to choose and did choose the possibility of His work revealed to us in His Word. But we cannot for this reason reckon on possibilities which are materially different.

— CD II/1, 542; EMPHASIS MINE

There is no higher truth of God above or behind Jesus Christ; there is no truth more complete than God's self-revelation. God has made Godself unreservedly known in Christ. Plainly, there is no God behind the back of Jesus Christ.

Pastorally, this means that we have no reason to be afraid of God. The abstract possibility that God is *not* like Jesus Christ, that there is another God hidden behind the revelation of God in Him, is deemed false. There is no such God for us to fear. There is only the God who makes Godself known as the gracious and loving God. Many imagine that God is a cosmic "hammer in the sky" just waiting for them to mess up and strike them with hot-blooded fury, but this is not the God and Father of Jesus Christ; this is a mythological projection of our greatest fears. Jesus Christ relieves our fears. God is not God against us, God is and forever will be God *for us*.

SIGNIFICANCE: Barth sets our thinking about God on a radically new course with the constant reminder that God is who He is in the person and work of Jesus Christ, that *this* is what God is like and that God is like *this*. Jesus Christ is God's full self-revelation, and we cannot look behind the back of Jesus Christ in search of a fearful, unknown, or unpredictable God. The fear that many Christians and non-Christians have about what God thinks of them, their worries that God might turn out to be some kind of an angry God, a God against us, is here removed. We have no God to fear who might possibly be *different* from the God revealed in Jesus Christ. There is no such God hidden behind the back of revelation. God is not God against us, the God and Father of Jesus Christ is unequivocally *God for us!* This insight has profound pastoral implications, beyond the obvious theological ones. We must not imagine any such God hidden behind the God revealed to us in Jesus Christ because no such God exists and is only a figment of our imagination. God is perfect love, and "perfect love casts out all fear" (1 John 4:18).

SIDEBAR: THE ONE WHO LOVES IN FREEDOM

I have said that I find Barth's rejection of a God hidden behind the back of Jesus Christ to be one of the more pastoral aspects of his thought, and here I want to expand upon that remark. With this, I also want to briefly introduce Barth's doctrine of God as the "One who loves in freedom" from *CD* II/1.

There is a terrible tendency in theology and preaching today to separate Jesus Christ from His Father, or from God more generally. What I mean is that Jesus is often presented as the "nice" side of God, full of grace and love, while the Father is the "mean" side of God, full of wrath and judgment. On account of Jesus' death, it is often implied the Father "tolerates" us. Only "in Jesus" does God love us in actuality. Jesus loves us and gives Himself to us, *but* the Father only cares about us *because* of Jesus and therefore only *superficially*.

Another way of saying this is that God's wrath and judgment are overcome by the love and grace of Jesus Christ, that Jesus "fixes" God's opinion about human beings in His life and death. In this scenario, God is reconciled to *Godself*(!), rather than the *world* being reconciled to God (see 2 Cor. 15:19). This is often not overtly stated, but it is far too often *implied* in our preaching and teaching. And while it is only *inadvertently* implied, it is implied nonetheless. Barth's rejection of a God hidden behind the back of Jesus Christ solves this problematic tendency.

Jesus tells us plainly, "Whoever has seen me *has seen* the Father" (John 14:9). There is no hidden God for us to fear behind the back of Jesus Christ; the gospel is not a sick cosmic joke or a twisted bait-and-switch ploy. There is no God different than the God who has made Godself known fully and unreservedly in Jesus Christ. In Him, the whole *fullness* of God dwells bodily (Col. 2:9).

We have not stressed this enough in our theology, and accordingly, our preaching has not made it clear enough. Many Christians today will readily say how much they know God loves them, but at the same time, if they're honest, they think maybe God doesn't *like* them very much. Maybe God only tolerates humanity? Perhaps, in the end, God will "turn His back" on us? Maybe on the last day, God will not look like Jesus after all? This is the dangerous downward spiral that results from mistrust in God's self-revelation. We must learn again from Barth to trust in Jesus Christ, to believe in Him as God's true revelation.

On a personal note, I can't tell you how many times I thought exactly like this without admitting it while I was growing up. For me, this dark, hidden God behind the back of Jesus manifested whenever I thought about the so-called "end times." As a young man, I was obsessed with the rapture and with timelines about what was going to happen when God's mercy ran out, when God finally gave up on humanity—yes, gave up on us! I honestly thought that was what would happen, if in more "spiritual" terms.

I believed that the second coming would manifest a God *different* from the God revealed in Jesus Christ. I was led to believe that even though God had acted graciously towards us in Jesus Christ, God's mercy will one day come to an end. The God who comes again will not be the God who came; God will return looking a lot more like the vengeful gods and goddesses of Greek mythology than like Jesus Christ.

This was my experience with the hidden God behind the back of Jesus Christ, the dark deity that plagued my dreams and infused my heart with fear. That is until I learned to think of God exclusively in terms of Jesus Christ; until I learned to trust divine revelation. Fear and anxiety have no place in a Christian doctrine of God. Barth's rejection of the hidden God behind the back of Jesus Christ is an incredibly pastoral doctrine with far-reaching implications, and I know it because I lived it.

The gospel is not a trick. There is no hidden God behind the back of Jesus Christ; God is who God has revealed Godself to be in Christ. We have to be clear about this fact if we are going to avoid the error of separating God from Jesus Christ. We must trust God's self-revelation, that God's Word is true.

One of the easiest ways to identify our lack of trust in divine revelation is whether or not we believe in a logical split between the "attributes" of God. For example, if we secretly think of God's love and wrath as *contradictions*. Christians sometimes struggle to reconcile their own (false) images of God with the God revealed in Jesus Christ. How can God be a God of wrath *and* love, of judgment *and* mercy? The answer we give determines how far we think exclusively of God in terms of Jesus Christ or give into the false notion of a God hidden behind His back. If we hold onto God's wrath as a hidden, dark side of God's love, we self-admittedly imagine a God hidden behind revelation.

This leads us to consider the doctrine of God in Barth's theology. While I won't present a complete overview of Barth's doctrine of God from *CD* II/1, I do want to note a few aspects of it as an example of how Barth rejected the hidden God behind Jesus Christ. Barth stresses that God is not divided in Godself, especially in God's "attributes." There is no God different in nature from Jesus Christ, held back or hidden behind God's self-revelation. With this Barth resolves our tendency to separate God from Jesus Christ, when we wrongly imagine that God the Father is the "bad cop" and Jesus is the "good cop." To see how this works out positively, we'll look at the unity of God's "perfections," specifically those of love and wrath, mercy and righteousness, and grace and holiness.

THE ONE WHO LOVES IN FREEDOM

Barth's statement about God as the "One who loves in freedom" is a brilliant way to distinguish God's determination to be *our* God, to bind and pledge Godself to us in Jesus Christ, without overlooking God's freedom to be God in Godself. This protects the doctrine of God from the dual error of over-emphasizing either the immanent Trinity (God in Godself) or the economic Trinity (God for us).

God is the One who *loves* (is for us in Christ) in *freedom* (is free in Godself). It is a brilliant formulation of the doctrine of God. Barth saw the importance of maintaining the unity of God's being for us and in Godself, while at once retaining the distinction.

Barth opts for the term "perfections" of God against the classic term "attributes" to distinguish God's way of being from humanity's. Therefore, we do not talk about God's "attributes" in the same way we talk about the attributes of friends or family members. We talk about the "perfections" of God to note this distinction between the being of God and of humanity. Thus, Barth notes that these perfections are not something God "has" but they are what God *is*.

> He does not possess this wealth [of perfections]. He Himself is this wealth. [...] He is Himself the perfect One in the abundance and variety of these His perfections.
>
> — CD II/1, 331

Barth is also careful to note the multiplicity and unity of God's perfections.

> Every distinction in God can be affirmed only in such a way as implies at the same time His unity and therefore the lack of essential discrepancy in what is distinguished. [...] Our doctrine therefore means that every individual perfection in God is nothing but God Himself and therefore nothing but every other divine perfection.
>
> — CD II/1, 333

PERFECTION WITHOUT CONTRADICTION

Returning to the issue at hand, we now see how God's perfections must be thought as both unique and united, multiple and inseparable. As an example, we will look at the perfections which are often divided: God's love and wrath, mercy and righteousness, and grace and holiness.

There are no *contradictory* perfections of God, but God exists in perfect unity and multiplicity. The unity of God's being excludes all contradiction even in multiplicity. Therefore, God's love *includes* God's wrath, God's mercy *includes* God's righteousness, and God's grace *includes* God's holiness—and vice versa. There is no dualistic split in God, but unity in multiplicity, multiplicity in unity.

The difficulty we have traditionally had with understanding this comes from the attempt to force *our definitions* of God's perfections onto the being of God without first allowing God's self-revelation to speak of and for Godself. *We* imagine that love cannot be wrath and wrath cannot be love; *we* believe that a merciful God cannot at once be righteous or that a righteous judge cannot be merciful; *we* imagine that holiness *excludes* grace rather than includes it. When we make ourselves the defining center of God's perfection, we will always inject contradictions which do not actually exist in God's being.

Barth writes:

It is not that we recognise and acknowledge the infinity, justice, wisdom, etc. of God because we already know from other sources what all this means and we apply it to God in an eminent sense, thus fashioning for ourselves an image of God after the pattern of our image of the world, i.e., in the last analysis after our own image.

— CD II/1, 333-4

The point here is that we cannot begin with ourselves defining God's perfections, but only with God's self-definition, that is, with Jesus Christ. God alone *defines* Godself just as God alone reveals Godself; God defines God's perfections. We may (rightly) imagine that God is a God of grace, but we cannot presuppose we know what grace means at all until we have learned it first from God's acts in Jesus Christ. In our minds, twisted by sin, we attempt to define God according to ourselves, but we are people of inherent disunity. Our definitions of love contradict our definitions of wrath, but God's does not. We may be slightly bipolar from time to time, turning from love and anger in a moment, but the God revealed in Jesus Christ is not bipolar; God is constant. We should not attempt to reconcile *our* image of God with Jesus Christ; we must leave behind our image of God and take up God's revelation of Godself. This is what it means to trust divine revelation: to lean not on our own understanding.

We cannot presuppose that we know what the word "God" means, and then try to make *our* definition of God better by adding Jesus into the mix. Barth reminds us that God alone defines God, and therefore that Jesus Christ is the only definition of God, the definition which destroys all of our own false definitions.

> Jesus Christ does not fill out and improve all the different attempts of man to think of God and to represent Him according to his own standard. But as the self-offering and self-manifestation of God He replaces and completely outbids those attempts, putting them in the shadows to which they belong.
>
> — CD I/2, 308

Barth's doctrine of God stresses the inherent unity and multiplicity of God as a central characteristic of our thinking about God's being in perfection. Barth rightly notes that the problem with so much of our theological speculation about the doctrine of God is that it begins with a God "in general" and only then turns to God in Triunity. Barth writes:

> The fundamental error of the whole earlier doctrine of God is reflected in this arrangement: first God's being in general, then His triune nature—with all the ambiguities and sources of error which must result from this sequence.
>
> — CD II/1, 348-9

Wonderfully, when we consider God properly, Barth reminds us, "God's revelation is first and last a Gospel, glad tidings, the word and deed of divine grace" (*CD* II/1, 349). God as the One who loves in freedom is God in unity and distinction, God in triunity, the God who makes Godself known exclusively and unreservedly in Jesus Christ. The revelation of *this* God is good news. We often present an image of God in *disunity* with Godself because we make ourselves the standard definition of God's perfections, but this is exactly what we cannot do. Barth solves this tendency with the rejection of the hidden God behind the back of Jesus Christ, and by the positive formation of the doctrine of God as the

One who loves in freedom. All of this continually forces us to lean not on our own understanding, but to trust in God's self-revelation; simply, to believe in Jesus Christ.

We now plainly see that it is a false-start to think of God with the assumption that God's love and wrath are a contradiction. With God, there simply *cannot* be any such contradiction. God's love is not without wrath and God's wrath is not without love. There is no isolated, arbitrary love of God nor is there an isolated, arbitrary wrath of God. Just as there is no Father without the Son and the Spirit, and no Son without the Father and the Spirit, so there is no perfection of God which stands alone without all the others. God is indivisibly *one* in diverse multiplicity.

Barth calls God's wrath the "fires of His love" (*CD* IV/1, 94). "If the fire of His wrath scorches us, it is because it is the fire of His wrathful love and not His wrathful hate" (*CD* III/2, 609). God's wrath consumes all that interferes with the purposes of God's love. God's wrath, therefore, is God's forceful *No* to all that stands against us, a no for the sake of a yes. God's wrath certainly does not mean God is "God-against-us." God's wrath is instead an expression of God's love for us, of God's self-determination to be God-for-us and with us in Jesus Christ. Wrath does not mean God ceases to be the God who loves us, but that God's love acts *for us* by removing our sin and our sin nature—since these are obstacles of God's love for us. Thus, wrath is the consuming fire of God's love. Barth writes:

> It is the holy fire of His Creator-love consuming and destroying the sin, rebellion and self-contradiction of man. Divine judgement in the biblical sense means that God vindicates Himself against man, but that in so doing He vindicates man against all that is alien and hostile to him. [...] It is not a No for its own sake, but a No for the sake of the Yes.
>
> — CD III/2, 32

What about God's grace and holiness? Barth writes, "The holiness of God consists in the unity of His judgement with His grace: God is holy because His grace judges and His judgement is gracious" (*CD* II/1, 363).

And further commenting on the wrongful divide between holiness and grace, Barth notes:

> If God's love is what is revealed to us in Jesus Christ, if Jesus Christ Himself is the revealed love of God, there is an end of the divorce between God's grace and holiness, and there remains to us only the recognition and adoration of Him who is both gracious and holy: gracious as He is holy and holy as He is gracious.
>
> — CD II/1, 367

What about God's mercy and righteousness? Barth writes:

> [B]ecause He is righteous God has mercy[.]
>
> — CD II/1, 387

> God's revelation in Jesus Christ supplies to this question the answer that the condemning and punishing righteousness of God is in itself and as such the depth and power and might of His mercy.
>
> — CD II/1, 393

There is no conflict within God's being; God's perfections are not *contradictions*. I have found that the wrongful division between these perfections of God—imagining by our definition of these perfections that God's being is in disunity—is the manifestation of our mistrust in God's self-revelation. We do not *really* trust that God is who God has revealed Godself to be in Jesus Christ. We imagine that God has held back from us, that there is a hidden God behind Jesus Christ. Barth's theology is a much-needed reminder that there is no such hidden God behind the back of Jesus Christ. God is who God has revealed Godself to be in Christ; God looks like Jesus.

SIDEBAR: NO HIDDEN WILL OF GOD

In the next chapter, we are going to look at Barth's doctrine of election. As a transition into that chapter, I want to briefly show how Barth's rejection of a hidden God behind Jesus Christ helps shape his doctrine of election.

Barth appreciated much about John Calvin's theology, but his disagreements with Calvin are no more strongly seen than in Barth's revisions to the doctrine of election. The primary reason why Barth felt he must reject Calvin's doctrine of election was because he thought Calvin had not listened to the Scriptures carefully enough; that instead, he had injected into the Scriptures his own experience with the world, his philosophical presuppositions. Barth's doctrine of election is his attempt to say what the Scriptures say about election more accurately; that is, to speak of election only in terms of Jesus Christ.

However, another essential element of this follows what we've just discussed. Barth rejects the idea of a hidden God behind revelation, and this includes the notion of a secret *will* in God which is somehow different than the will of God revealed in Jesus Christ. Accordingly, Barth insists that when we discuss the doctrine of election we are not speaking of an abstract God who decides to elect some individuals over others, but of *Jesus Christ,* who is both the electing and elected One. Only with Jesus Christ in mind can we rightly understand God's gracious election.

Barth highlights the problem with Calvin's doctrine:

> The thought of the election [for Calvin] becomes necessarily the thought of the will and decision of God which are hidden somewhere in the heights or depths *behind Jesus Christ* and behind God's revelation. The first and last question in respect of the relationship between God and man brings us face to face with a God who is above and beyond Jesus Christ and with a relationship which is independent of Jesus Christ.
>
> — CD II/2, 64; EMPHASIS MINE

This is the logical conclusion of asserting a will of God hidden behind the back of Jesus Christ. Because of the refusal to speak of a will of God higher than or hidden behind the back of Jesus Christ, Barth speaks about election and forms his doctrine in such a way that it is the doctrine of Jesus Christ as the electing God and elected man.

In the place of an "absolute decree" or hidden will of God inherent to Calvin's doctrine, Barth re-centers the doctrine of election on Jesus Christ:

> It must be shown, then, that it is Jesus Christ Himself who occupies this place. It must be shown that in Him we have to do not only with very man but with very God. It must be shown that in Him we have to do not only with elected man but with electing, the truly and freely electing God.
>
> — CD II/2, 75

And directly, Barth writes:

> The will of God *is* Jesus Christ, and this will is known to us in the revelation of Jesus Christ. If we acknowledge this, if we seriously accept Jesus Christ as the content of this will, then we cannot seek any other will of God, either in heaven or earth, either in time or eternity. This will is God's will.
>
> — CD II/2, 157

This rejection of a hidden will of God is one of the driving forces behind Barth's doctrine of election and one of the major reasons why Barth rejects Calvin's horrible decree of double-predestination. We'll return to this error and examine it more fully in the sidebar on "Limited Atonement and Calvin's Horrible Decree" (chapter 7).

5

THE GOD OF ELECTION

Summary: The doctrine of election is the "sum of the Gospel"; it is wholly good news. The content of God's gracious election is the person of Jesus Christ, God's self-determination to be God-for-us, as both the electing God and elected human being. It is primarily a doctrine about God and only as such about humanity elected in Christ.

In Barth's own words:

The doctrine of election is the sum of the Gospel because of all words that can be said or heard it is the best: that God elects man; that God is for man too the One who loves in freedom. It is grounded in the knowledge of Jesus Christ because He is both the electing God and elected man in One. It is part of the doctrine of God because originally God's election of man is a predestination not merely of man but of Himself. Its function is to bear basic testimony to eternal, free and unchanging grace as the beginning of all the ways and works of God.

— CD II/2, 3

Thus the simplest form of the dogma [of election] may be divided at

once into two assertions that Jesus Christ is the electing God, and that
He is also elected man.

— CD II/2, 103

The content of God's Word is his free, undeserved Yes to the whole
human race, in spite of all human unreasonableness and corruption.

— EVANGELICAL THEOLOGY, 79

SECONDARY QUOTES:

But the question, 'To whom does election apply?' is, from Barth's point
of view, a secondary question. What is primary is the question, 'Who is
the God who elects and what does a knowledge of this God tell us about
the nature of election?' Barth's revolution is finally a revolution in the
doctrine of God[.]

— BRUCE MCCORMACK: "GRACE AND BEING," THE
CAMBRIDGE COMPANION TO KARL BARTH, 93

There is no other God of election behind God-in-Jesus Christ.

— ROBERT JENSON: ALPHA AND OMEGA, 144

Barth does not see the doctrine of election as presenting us with an
abstract electing God or with *abstract* elect men, but it presents us
'concretely with the confession of Jesus Christ as the electing God as the
elect man.'

— G. C. BERKOUWER: THE TRIUMPH OF GRACE, 98

INTRODUCTION

Here we turn to what is without a doubt one of the most discussed
aspects of Barth's theology, the doctrine of election. Personally, this is
where I began with Barth. I took an interest in his theology out of

curiosity for his doctrine of election. The significance of Barth's revision has already been stated by many, so in this chapter, we will try and give a thorough and straightforward introduction to how Barth forms and develops this doctrine.

ELECTION AS GOOD NEWS

Barth begins by calling the doctrine of election the "sum of the gospel." It is the message of grace, the good news of God's will towards humanity. And as such, "It is not a mixed message of joy and terror, salvation and damnation" (*CD* II/2, 13). There is no ambiguity in God's gracious election. It is not a word of "Yes… but" or of "maybe." No, the doctrine of election is God's unequivocal and resounding "Yes!" to the human race. There is no confusion or speculation regarding God's will towards us in Jesus Christ. God's will is not a hidden will but a revealed will. As grace, election is God's love towards us, and as God's love, it is at once God's freedom. Election is, therefore, God's free and loving self-determination to be *God for us* in Jesus Christ, to be our God and for us to be God's people. It is therefore primarily a statement *about the electing God* and only as such is it a statement about humanity elected in Christ.

Barth places the doctrine of election within the doctrine of God (*CD* II). The point here is that election cannot become an abstract, philosophical idea. Election is rightly understood only in the light of who God has revealed Godself to be in Jesus Christ. There is no abstract electing deity or abstract elected humanity, but Jesus Christ. God has revealed Godself in Christ to be the One who loves in freedom, and *this* God alone is the electing God.

Barth's doctrine of election removes the haunting, speculative question: is God really for me? Answering unequivocally, Yes! Because election is not about an abstract God or abstract humanity; it is a doctrine which speaks of Jesus Christ, the electing and elected One. Therefore, the doctrine of election is not a speculative theory, but the positive assertion of God's will to be for us and not against us. It is God's unequivocal Yes to humanity.

There is no dark, hidden, absolute decree in God; there is only the grace and love of God towards us in Him. Election means the *beginning* of all God's ways and works is *grace*. The speculative tendency in other doctrines of election is here removed at its root. Because God is who God is for us in Jesus Christ, we cannot speak of any higher or greater will of God that is not found in Christ. God's gracious election is good news of great joy for the whole world; it is the sum of the gospel.

JESUS CHRIST: ELECTING GOD, ELECTED MAN

Election is a statement about God, and only as such is it a statement about humanity. Election is God's self-determination to be God for us in Jesus Christ, to be the electing God; and at once it is the determination of human beings to be us-for-God in Jesus Christ, to be the elected people. Election in the simplest form *is* the person of Jesus Christ who is at once God and man, at once the electing God and the elected human being. Simply, Jesus Christ *is* election.

While Barth takes issue with Calvin's doctrine of double-predestination for creating a speculative God of a twofold decree, he does not entirely reject the notion of double-predestination. Instead, for Barth double predestination is the election *and rejection* of Jesus Christ, it is God's self-double-predestination. It is not the election of some human beings and the rejection of others; it is both the election *and* rejection of the one man Jesus Christ.

For God to say *Yes* to humanity, God must at once say *Yes* and *No* to Godself. God takes up our cause as God's own in Jesus Christ, bearing the weight of our sin in Christ's suffering and death on the cross. Christ bears our condition as sinners, taking our place, living and dying for us. At the center of Barth's doctrine of election is the love of God in self-humiliation on the cross. Just as Jesus Christ is the one true elected human being, so Jesus Christ is the one and only true *rejected* human being. God says *No* to the sinful creature in Jesus Christ, putting to death the old nature in Him, but it was for the sake of saying *Yes* to the creature. By taking the effects of sin upon Himself, Jesus Christ acts as the one reprobate, the only rejected human being, for the sake of the election of all in Him. On the cross, Jesus Christ bore our rejection.

Barth writes:

> He who is in the one person the electing God and the one elect man is as the rejecting God, the God who judges sin in the flesh, in His own

person the one rejected man, the Lamb which bears the sin of the world that the world should no longer have to bear it or be able to bear it, that it should be radically and totally taken away from it.

— CD IV/1, 237

This passage is in the heart of Barth's doctrine of reconciliation, under the heading (§59.2), "The Judge Judged in Our Place." Jesus Christ takes our place as those who rightly deserve rejection and judgment, and in a gracious divine exchange, we take part in Christ's election as He takes part in our rejection. Christ suffers the end of the old creation and posits the beginning of the new. God says *No* so that God can speak an unequivocal *Yes*.

It is important to see Barth's doctrine of election in conjunction with both the doctrine of God on the one hand and the doctrine of reconciliation on the other. Both play integral roles in how Barth forms the doctrine of election.

In a beautiful summary of this self-double-predestination of God, Barth writes:

That the elected man Jesus had to suffer and die means no more and no less than that in becoming man God makes Himself responsible for man who became His enemy, and that He takes upon Himself all the consequences of man's action—his rejection and his death. This is what is involved in the self-giving of God. This is the radicalness of His grace.

— CD II/2, 124

The doctrine of election is such a central issue for Barth that even in one of the final volumes of the *Church Dogmatics* it was essential.

For man's election is his election in Jesus Christ, the Son of God, whom the Father, and He Himself, has not elected for this or that man but for all men, and who has not elected this or that man but all men for Himself. In this twofold election He has taken to Himself and away from them all the rejection which applies to all men as sinners and separates them from God. Not in and of himself, but in Jesus Christ as the eternal beginning of all God's ways and works, no man is rejected, but all are elected in Him to their justification, their sanctification and also their vocation.

— CD IV/3.2, 484

THE ELECTION OF THE COMMUNITY AND THE INDIVIDUAL

Election is primarily the election of Jesus Christ, but in His election, there is included the election of all humanity. Barth stresses however that this does not first mean *individuals*, but the election of the *community*. First Israel and then the Church. However, at the same time, Barth stresses that within the community the individual is not lost or forgotten. Both emphases are present here as Barth works out the practical implications of the doctrine of election. The election of human beings in Jesus Christ is first the election of Christ's community, the Church, which is His earthy-historical existence.

It will be helpful first to examine a unique aspect of this doctrine. For Barth, the *human response* of obedience to God is also included in the election of Jesus Christ. Election is not a one-sided decree, but a covenant which is upheld by both covenant partners in Him. When we talk about the community and the individual affected by God's election of Christ, we are talking about a total covenant fulfilled in Him. Election, therefore, is not the *possibility* of becoming God's people or the offer of a partial relationship in which you must uphold your part of the deal. No, it is clear that what Barth has in mind here is that when we take part in the election of Jesus Christ, we take part in God's relationship with Jesus Christ, *and* His relationship as a man with God on our behalf. God's decision is not conditioned by a complementary human decision. God's decision, the election of Jesus Christ, *includes* the human decision. Jesus Christ acted in our place as the one true elected human, not merely as a passive recipient of election, but as an active and obedient recipient. In Him, the decision to be God's people has been made on our behalf. In Him, the covenant from both the side of God and the side of humanity is upheld and fulfilled.

God does not treat us like puppets. When Jesus Christ takes up our human response to God—our obedience and gratitude—as His own, we attain *freedom* to truly be God's people, to elect the God who has already elected us in Christ. Within Christ's election, we attain this freedom and not apart from it. We are made free in the freedom of God; we share in God's freedom. There is no contradiction between God's sovereign will and the freedom of human beings, quite the opposite is true. Human beings are free only *in* God's will, in obedience to God's will, and in being who they are created to be in Jesus Christ. Therefore, Barth writes, "Between the sovereignty of God and the freedom of the creature there is no contradiction" (*CD* III/3, 166). God's gracious election in Jesus Christ establishes and creates *true* human freedom; it does not negate freedom. To be free is to be in fellowship with God in and through the fellowship of Jesus Christ.

That being said, we'll now turn to how Barth deals with the election of the community and the individual. First, Barth presents a lengthy discussion of Israel and the Church as the two forms of the one community of God. The former's existence being in hearing God's Word, and the latter's in believing; the former's existence as being which is passing away, and the latter's as becoming new. There is only one community of God, but Barth distinguishes between Israel and the Church in this way: "This one community of God in its form as Israel has to serve the representation of divine judgement, in its form as the Church the representation of divine mercy" (*CD* II/2, 195). The community is ultimately elected for the sake of all humanity. In its two forms, Israel and the Church, Christ is present for the sake of the world.

Next Barth turns to individuals elected within the community. His emphasis on the community does not negate the importance of the individual elected in Jesus Christ, but as the individual is elected in Him, they are at once elected to the community. The point here is that there is no individual election *in abstracto,* in isolation, apart from the community. Election takes place within the community, within the people of God. The Church, as the Body of Christ, is essential for election *in* Christ.

Election recognizes the individual within humanity as a whole. Neither stark individualism nor the total loss of individuality can be present in our thinking about this. Both aspects are important and belong together: both the community in which the individual belongs and the individuals that make up the community.

Now, there is an important clarification to make. Barth is well aware of the difficulties in saying that all human beings have been elected to a fulfilled covenant in Jesus Christ. In saying this Barth does not give into a fantasy, as if he imagines all humanity to be now perfect, obedient Christians. Instead, Barth carefully understands that even while the individual is ultimately elected in Jesus Christ, they may still reject their election and live like a reprobate, even in spite of their election. They may live in falsehood. God's will towards such an individual has not changed (because it cannot), nor is their election revoked (because it cannot be), but such an individual rejects their own election without negating God's gracious will towards them. In rejecting this, they are refusing their very basis for existence, their very nature as God's creature determined for fellowship with God in Jesus Christ. As such, it is the *impossible possibility* of their existence, it is their self-contradicting sin, which causes them to go against their very nature as God's elect by pretending to be what they are not. To be a reprobate before God is now a contradiction in terms. It is to live in falsehood. In Barth's own words, "[T]his choice of the godless man is void; [...] he belongs eternally to Jesus Christ and therefore is not rejected, but elected by God in Jesus Christ" (*CD* II/2, 306).

Barth writes further:

> [The godless person] cannot reverse or change the eternal decision of God—by which He regards, considers and wills man, not in his isolation over against Him, but in His Son Jesus. Man can certainly keep on lying (and does so); but he cannot make truth falsehood. He can certainly rebel (he does so); but he can accomplish nothing which abolishes the choice of God. He can certainly flee from God (he does so), but he cannot escape Him. He can certainly hate God and be hateful to God (he does and is so); but he cannot change into its opposite the eternal love of God which triumphs even His hate. [...] He may let go of God, but God does not let go of him.
>
> — CD II/2, 317

All human beings are graciously elected to fellowship with God in

Jesus Christ, and therefore each person is irrevocably loved and included in God's grace. No matter how radically they attempt to reject their own election, they cannot change God's will. Their ability to reject God is null and void in Christ's obedience to His Father on their behalf, in God's election of Jesus Christ and of His human election of God. The choice to be free from God, to be finally and ultimately rejected by God, is a choice taken away from all humanity in Him. The *only* rejected individual is God in Christ who suffered our rejection for the sake of all humanity. Not everyone will live their lives as the elect of God, but all are elected in Him irrespective of their belief in it. Election is *the* fact of our existence.

This is the sum of the Gospel. God is so for us and for all humanity that God has determined not to be God without us, God has elected Godself to be our God and for us to be God's people. In Jesus Christ, we see God's gracious election: the electing God and the elected man. In Him, the community and the individual are included in the covenant of grace.

Barth's doctrine of election is without a doubt one of the most complicated subjects he addresses. It presents an entirely new framework for thought, and for that reason, it can be difficult to take in all at once. Barth is working here with a paradox—*the mystery of iniquity*—in discussing the election of the individual. Sin is fundamentally an irrational issue: an *impossible possibility*. Barth's careful treatment of election and the individual's rejection of their election is the attempt to say something constructive about the irrationality of human iniquity in the face of God's grace. Barth retains the fact of God's election of all humanity in Jesus Christ, and of the human response to that election at once fulfilled in Jesus Christ, yet acknowledges the mystery of an individual's rejection of their election. Keeping this paradox in mind is helpful while reading how Barth discusses the implications of the doctrine of election.

In closing, I want to stress the importance of seeing this as an entirely new framework of thought. The former ways of understanding election in their Calvinistic or semi-Pelagian character are shattered and overcome in Barth's doctrine of election.

Thomas F. Torrance offers an insightful analogy to describe this new theological framework. He compares Barth's theology to the framework-shattering science of Albert Einstein. Sir Isaac Newton had posited a closed, mechanistic world-system, where God can only be a kind of clock-maker who set the world into motion but is no longer active in it. That gave rise to deism and determinism. Then Albert Einstein radically shattered this closed system, this mechanistic worldview, with his theory of general relativity. It is a new framework which radically changes the way we think about the world.

No less radically, Karl Barth's theology, especially here in the doctrine of election, shatters our former ways of thinking. The common dead-lock discussion between theology as God's determination or as humanity's determination (Calvinism vs. Arminianism) is reconstructed and overcome as a false dualism. No longer is it necessary to speak of God in this way. We are free to reach a better understanding of God's self-revelation in Jesus Christ, which supersedes all our systematic constructions. We must be cautious not to create a dead *concept* out of a living *person*. The doctrine of election is particularly difficult at first because it presents us with this new framework of thought. It's like going from a Newtonian to an Einsteinian worldview. But it is worth taking the time to study and understand it for exactly that reason.

SIGNIFICANCE: Barth's doctrine of election removes the fearful tendency of imagining that God somehow might not be for us, that perhaps God has some higher and crueler motive for creating the world, and that perhaps we are not the objects of God's love but the objects of God's anger. Barth takes this feeble "maybe" which predominates a majority of our conversations surrounding election and predestination, and shatters it with God's resounding Yes to us in Jesus Christ. In Him, we are the recipients of that Yes which is never No or even Yes and No, but always an unequivocal word of affirmation. God has always loved you and has always willed to be your God and to have you as His child. Nothing can change God's gracious will for election. The beginning of all God's ways and works is grace. We have confidence and certainty in Jesus Christ, not because we ourselves have obtained such confidence, but because Jesus Christ is the source and foundation of our hope.

SERMON: PREACHING ELECTION

A sermon that Barth preached to prisoners in Basel offers an accessible summary of his doctrine of election. The title of the sermon is "Teach us to Number Our Days," on Psalm 90:12. Barth writes:

> What happened in the death of Jesus did not happen against us, but *for us*. What took place was not an act of God's wrath against man. Quite the opposite holds true. Because in the one Jesus God loved us from all eternity—truly all of us—because he has elected himself to be our dear Father and has elected us to become his dear children whom he wants to save and draw unto him, therefore he has in the one Jesus written off, rejected, nailed to a cross and killed our old man who, as impressibly as he may dwell and spook about in us, is not our true self. God so acted for our sake.

> — Deliverance to the Captives, 122-3

This is a short but succinct summary of Barth's doctrine of election. While it certainly lacks the thoroughness of Barth's treatment of election in *CD* II/2, it is an insightful example of how Barth *preached* the doctrine of election more than just how he taught it.

Note a few things with this sermon. First, the context of this pronouncement is the death of Jesus Christ. Christ's cross is central to Barth's doctrine of election, too. Jesus Christ, as both the electing God and elected man, is at once the *one and only* rejected man. God, therefore, acts *for us* in Christ's death.

Second, Barth describes God's love from all eternity as God's *self-determining* love. God elected *Godself* and only then elected humanity *in Christ.* God determined Godself to be our God and for us to be His people.

And finally, God's will to be our God and for us to be God's beloved children results in the crucifixion of our old nature, which has been rejected and destroyed in Christ's death. While that old nature might still "spook" us like a ghost, it is not our true nature anymore. We are the elect children of God.

Barth concludes this thought by highlighting the new nature that is put forth in Jesus' resurrection. He writes:

> Because the old man—you know him well enough—has already been extinguished in the death of Jesus, because you may no longer be this old man, because your own case has been disposed of by the power of Jesus' death, therefore you yourself are now the new man, loved by God, chosen, saved and accepted by him who has said to you and will say to you his divine 'yes'.
>
> — IBID., 123

ALL

In another sermon, Barth preaches on the universality of the gospel, based on Romans 11:32. It is yet another example of the confidence we have in God's gracious will towards us in Jesus Christ. Barth writes:

> God has mercy on us. He says 'yes' to us, he wills to be on our side, to be our God against all odds. [...] Contrary to human mercy even in its kindest expression, God's mercy is almighty. It is almightily saving and helpful. It brings light, peace and joy. We

need not be afraid that it might be limited or have strings attached. His 'yes' is unequivocal, never to be reversed into 'no'.

— DELIVERANCE TO THE CAPTIVES, 87

Here Barth highlights what I believe to be one of the key pastoral benefits of his doctrine of election: the unequivocal Yes of God. We are not up against Calvin's hidden and mysterious "horrible decree," nor are we up against a hidden God behind the back of Jesus Christ. In Him, we see God's unreserved, valid Yes: God's limitless affirmation of our humanity. God's eternal lovingkindness revealed is in the life, death, and resurrection of Jesus Christ. In short, we find in this the good news that God is not God against us, but is in Godself before all time *God for us*.

SIDEBAR: UNIVERSALISM

Barth's doctrine of election naturally raises the question of universalism. If we confess that all are elected in Jesus Christ and through Him made covenant partners with God, doesn't that automatically mean the confession of universal salvation? Barth's response is unique. Many have tried to force Barth to say either yes or no to the question of universalism, but in reality, he says *both* yes and no. Barth argues for the negation of dogmatic universalism *and* dogmatic particularism. We'll look at three key examples from *CD* II/2, *The Humanity of God,* and *CD* IV/3.1 in which Barth directly addressed this question.

CD II/2

Many have falsely claimed that it is a logical necessity, following the doctrine of election, for Barth to affirm universal redemption. But Barth explicitly denies this is the case. Under the heading, "The Determination of the Elect" from §35 in *CD* II/2, Barth explains why such a conclusion should be rejected. Essentially, Barth argues that the extent to which the "circle" of salvation includes only some or all of humanity is determined solely by Jesus Christ; universalism is a question only God can and one day will answer in freedom. Barth writes:

It is [Christ's] concern what is to be the final extent of the circle. If we are to respect the freedom of divine grace, we cannot venture the statement that it must and will finally be coincident with the world of man as such (as in the doctrine of the so-called *apokatastasis* [universalism]). No such right or necessity can legitimately be deduced. Just as the gracious God does not need to elect or call any single man, so He does not need to elect or call all mankind. His election and calling do not give rise to any historical metaphysics, but only to the necessity of attesting them on the ground that they have taken place in Jesus Christ and His community. But, again, in grateful recognition of the grace of the divine freedom we cannot venture the opposite statement that there cannot and will not be this final opening up and enlargement of the circle of election and calling. Neither as the election of Jesus Christ, the election of His community, nor the election of the individual do we know the divine election of grace as anything other than a decision of His loving-kindness. We would be developing an opposing historical metaphysics if we were to try to attribute any limits [...] to the loving kindness of God.

— CD II/2, 417-8

Barth considers both alternatives, either the limitation of God's loving-kindness (the absolute rejection of universalism) or our attempt at answering a question only God can answer (the total acceptance of universalism), to be abstract speculation and therefore of having no part in the task of dogmatics. Fundamentally, Barth sees the question of universalism as one that only God in freedom can and will answer. Therefore it is forbidden for us either to limit God's love by declaring salvation only for *some* (by rejecting universalism) or the opposite, to force God's free love into including *all* in that circle (by affirming it as a fact).

THE HUMANITY OF GOD

This same line of reasoning is further clarified in Barth's small volume,

The Humanity of God. Barth asks, in the light of God's unequivocal affirmation of humanity:

> Does this mean universalism? I wish here to make only three short observations, in which one is to detect no position for or against that which passes among us under this term.
>   1. One should not surrender himself in any case to the panic which this word seems to spread abroad, before informing himself exactly concerning its possible sense or non-sense.

> — THE HUMANITY OF GOD, 61

In other words, let's not be too hasty in rejecting universalism as complete nonsense, *or* from the opposite perspective, as the only possible answer, as complete sense. Universalism shouldn't create an immediate fear-based reaction from us. I can't help but think here of the American Evangelical community and their response to the mere *suggestion* of universalism found in Rob Bell's now infamous book, *Love Wins*. Barth would tell us not to panic at such a suggestion. Barth continues:

> 2. One should at least be stimulated by the passage, Colossians 1:19[-20], which admittedly states that God has determined through His Son as His image and as the first-born of the whole Creation to 'reconcile all things (τὰ πάντα) to himself,' to consider whether the concept could not perhaps have a good meaning. The same can be said of parallel passages.

> — IBID., 61-2

In other words, Barth points to Colossians 1:19-20 as a Scripture which, among others, should at the very least open us up to the *possibility* of universal reconciliation. We cannot be so quick to discount such a passage or to limit its importance.

And finally, here is Barth's third and critical point:

> 3. One question should for a moment be asked, in view of the 'danger' with which one may see this concept gradually

surrounded. What of the 'danger' of the eternally skeptical-critical theologian who is ever and again suspiciously questioning, because fundamentally always legalistic and therefore in the main morosely gloomy? Is not his presence among us currently more threatening than that of the unbecomingly cheerful indifferentism or even antinomianism, to which one with a certain understanding of universalism could in fact deliver himself? This much is certain, that we have no theological right to set any sort of limits to the loving-kindness of God which has appeared in Jesus Christ. Our theological duty is to see and understand it as being still greater than we had seen before.

— Ibid., 62

His last two sentences are critical. Who are we to limit the love God has for sinners in Jesus Christ? Not only is it more cheerful to have hope in this possibility, but it is a serious error to absolutely reject it by presuming that God's love inherently has such a limit. We limit God's love and freedom if we have determined ahead of time in our minds to exclude the possibility of universalism. We may wonder about this question, but we have no theological justification to limit God's love. Barth is right, "Our theological duty is to see and understand [God's love] as being still greater than we had seen before."

This answer is characteristic of how Barth addressed the question of universalism. With the freedom of God in mind, Barth opposed both *dogmatic* universalism and the *dogmatic* rejection of universalism (i.e., particularism). This is one of the reasons why Barth was notoriously difficult to pin down. This (non-)answer was Barth's typical reply when asked about universalism: "I don't believe in universalism, but I do believe in Jesus Christ, the reconciler of all" (Busch, 394). Or Barth would cleverly say:, "I don't teach it, but I don't not teach it."

In this sense we could argue, being careful not to place any labels on Barth, that he was a kind of "hopeful" universalist, who at once rejected the logical *necessity* of universalism but at the same time rejected the logical necessity of particularism. For Barth, ultimately the question of universalism is one that only God can and will answer, and we risk the prideful attempt of "playing God" whenever we try to answer it ourselves.

This is *God's* question, not ours. God, as the One who loves *in freedom*, will one day answer it. We may hope for it, but we cannot teach it as dogmatic truth—either in the affirmative or the negative.

CD IV/3.1

We'll now examine one final place where Barth makes a similar twofold response to the question of universalism. This comes from the end of *CD* IV/3.1 (literally on the last page), under the heading "The Condemnation of Man" in §70. I want to bring this passage to your attention because here Barth explains why we must confess that there remains the *possibility* of some being eternally condemned, just as much as there remains the possibility of none being condemned. If this passage is understood correctly, the claim that universalism is a logical necessity of Barth's thought would be removed.

For Barth, we are up against the mystery of iniquity, of sin and evil, which he has called the "impossible possibility" or the "ontological impossibility." Sin as human falsehood, like lying, is our attempt to turn *truth* into *untruth*. This is Barth's doctrine of sin in *CD* IV/3.1. Barth discusses the *condemnation* of the individual who lives in this impossibility, who attempts to turn the truth of their reconciliation in Jesus Christ into an untruth—thereby condemning themselves. It is in *this* sense that there remains the possibility of a populated hell. These individuals who pervert the truth of God into falsehood may suffer the consequences of their falsehood, and therefore suffer the judgment of God which they no longer deserve. Their choice to live in untruth may ultimately end in their condemnation. This is the self-contradicting, impossible possibility of condemnation against God's unequivocal affirmation of their existence in the election of Jesus Christ.

In this context, Barth writes, "To the man who persistently tries to change the truth into untruth, God does not owe eternal patience and therefore deliverance" (*CD* IV/3.1, 477). In other words, God does not owe the sinner who persists in their own self-condemnation any hope of final deliverance. But, in spite of the fact that God does not *have* to deliver and turn towards the sinner with patience and mercy, Barth notes:

There is no good reason why we should forbid ourselves, or be forbidden, openness to the possibility that in the reality of God and man in Jesus Christ there is contained much more than we might expect and therefore the supremely unexpected withdrawal of that final threat, i.e., that in the truth of this reality there might be contained the super-abundant promise of the final deliverance of all men. To be more explicit, there is no good reason why we should not be open to this possibility.

— CD IV/3.1, 477-8

We cannot *count* on this possibility, but we must hope and pray for it. Barth continues:

If we are certainly forbidden to count on this as though we had a claim to it, as though it were not supremely the work of God to which man can have no possible claim, we are surely commanded more definitely to hope and pray for it as we may do already on this side of this final possibility, i.e., to hope and pray cautiously and yet distinctly that, in spite of everything which may seem quite conclusively to proclaim the opposite, His compassion should not fail, and that in accordance with His mercy which is 'new every morning' He 'will not cast off for ever' (La. 3:22f, 31).

— CD IV/3.1, 478

The critical context for understanding Barth's answer to universalism is *prayer*. We are commanded to hope and pray for the salvation of all because universalism is a question we have no right to answer for ourselves. If we demand a definitive answer to the question of universalism, we try to become like God. But in prayer, we humble ourselves and rightly acknowledge God's goodness and freedom to save. Barth commends the latter against the former; prayer takes precedence over the demand for certainty. Therefore, Barth refuses to answer the question that only God can and will answer, the question of universalism. This conclusion is not indefiniteness or a contradiction, but an expression of Barth's prayerful humility before God's freedom.

THE TENSION OF SCRIPTURE

Bruce McCormack helpfully describes Barth's response to universalism as the attempt to remain faithful to *what* the Scriptures actually say on this issue and how they say it; that is, to speak of the *tension* between history and eschatology. It is Barth's dedication to the Scripture which ultimately stands behind this twofold answer. Barth was attentive to the fact that the Scriptures hold this paradox, this tension: on one side there is scriptural hope for universal reconciliation, and on the other hand, there is the possibility of a populated hell. Where most try to *resolve* this tension, Barth allows the tension to stand.

McCormack writes:

> I think there are good and sufficient reasons *not* to eliminate the tension but to allow it to stand [...]. I also think that both traditional Calvinist and traditional Arminian exegesis misfire— and misfire at precisely the same point. Both treat the propositions found in Scripture as standing in a strict logical relationship to one another, so that any tension that might exist among them must finally be regarded as a contradiction—which would obviously threaten biblical authority. My own view is that the tension I have identified is not rightly understood as a contradiction. Rather, it is a function of the tension between history and eschatology, between time and eternity, between certitudes and mysteries, between what may be said with great definiteness and what must finally be left open-ended and unresolved.
>
> — KARL BARTH AND AMERICAN EVANGELICALISM, 230

Barth speaks this twofold response not because he was afraid of the term universalism (he warns against such a reaction), nor because he was secretly a universalist and spoke in code (some have tried to claim Barth as a "closet" universalist!). Instead, Barth speaks about universalism in this way because *this is the way the Scriptures speak of it.*

We can and should *hope* and *pray* for universal reconciliation, but we cannot teach it as dogma. To ultimately teach it as either fact or to reject it as heresy is to attempt to resolve this tension within the Scriptures, either towards one position or the other. This makes human beings, ourselves, and our logic the determining factor in this answer, and not God in freedom. It is in this sense our prideful attempt to play God as we try to resolve this tension because we attempt to take away God's freedom to answer only what God can and will answer by answering it ourselves.

6

CREATION AND THE COVENANT

SUMMARY: Creation is the *external* basis of the covenant of grace, and the covenant of grace is the *internal* basis of creation. In other words, God created the world for the sake of the covenant, and specifically for the sake of Jesus Christ, so that the creature might be reconciled to God and have fellowship with God in Him. The reconciliation and redemption of the creature was not an afterthought. Barth develops a doctrine of creation, evil, and of human beings all in the light of Jesus Christ and His saving work. The internal basis, the *why* of the creation, is the covenant; the external basis, the *what* of the covenant, is creation. Thus creation is *benefit*, God's Yes to humanity.

IN BARTH'S OWN WORDS:

For Christ who seems to come second, really comes first, and Adam who seems to come first really comes second. In Christ the relationship between the one and the many is original, in Adam it is only a copy of that original. Our relationship to Adam depends for its reality on our relationship to Christ. And that means, in practice, that to find the true and essential nature of man we have to look not to Adam the fallen man, but to Christ in whom what is fallen has been cancelled and what was original has been restored. We have to correct and interpret what we know of Adam by what we know of Christ, because Adam is only true man in so far as he reflects and points to the original humanity of Christ.

— CHRIST AND ADAM: MAN AND HUMANITY IN ROMANS
5, 74-5

Creation is grace: a statement at which we should like best to pause in reverence, fear and gratitude. [...] The world came into being, it was created and sustained by the little child that was born in Bethlehem, by the Man who died on the Cross of Golgotha, and the third day rose again. *That* is the Word of creation, by which all things were brought into being. That is where the *meaning* of creation comes from[.]

— DOGMATICS IN OUTLINE, 54, 58

But if Jesus Christ is the content and form of the first and eternal Word of God, then that means further that the beginning of all things, of the being of all men and of the whole world, even the divine willing of creation, is preceded by God's *covenant* with man as its basis and purpose.

— CD IV/1, 53

The covenant is the goal of creation and creation the way of the covenant.

— CD III/1, 97

SECONDARY QUOTES:

Man in creation is thus already entirely and completely under the *grace* of God, and thus *in an eminent way.*

— HANS KÜNG: JUSTIFICATION, 20

A theology of creation is, in the deepest sense, a theology of salvation and cannot be developed apart from a context of faith. Creation is, as it were, the first work of the triune God and as such is not yet a reconciliation or a consummation. Reconciliation and consummation, however, do have in creation their *anticipation,* and in that sense they do begin with creation.

— IBID., 11

For Barth, Jesus Christ, the Savior of sinners, precedes creation and is its basis.

— ROBERT W. JENSON: ALPHA AND OMEGA, 93

THE COVENANT OF GRACE; CHRIST AND ADAM

Human beings in creation exist to be loved by God, to be *God's* creature. Creation is the "external basis" of the covenant, and the covenant is the "internal basis" of creation. This means the covenant, God's will to be reconciled and in fellowship with the creature, is the *why* of creation. Creation, as the theater for the covenant, is the *what* of creation. Creation is, therefore, the formal content, and the covenant the material content, of the doctrine of creation. Before we discuss the details of Barth's doctrine of creation, this relationship will be our focus.

Reconciliation is presupposed in the creation of the world. Today, when the gospel is preached it is far too often said that God created a perfect world which humanity later messed up and therefore forced God into a *reactionary* mode against sin. The life, death, and resurrection of Jesus Christ become an *afterthought,* God's "plan B." Barth clearly rejects this notion right from the start. Reconciliation was not an afterthought. God's will to be in fellowship (in a covenant) with God's creature is the *why* of creation. The covenant of grace is "plan A," and there has never been a plan B. Creation took place *because* God willed the event of reconciliation; because God willed to be gracious to humanity in Jesus Christ.

In the last chapter, we looked at the doctrine of election, which tells us that the beginning of all God's ways and works is *grace.* Barth forms the doctrine of creation in a similar way; God creates *to be gracious* to the creature. God creates for the sake of Jesus Christ and us in Him, for the sake of reconciliation. God willed before all time to become a man in

Jesus Christ, to reconcile the world to God in His life, death, and resurrection. Reconciliation and the covenant to which it belongs is not a *reaction* to sin, but the presupposition of creation.

Barth's task here is to show that creation is not just a doctrine about an abstract God creating abstract humanity. Yet again Barth is insistent upon removing all abstractions from our thinking. Instead, he stresses that this is the *Christian* doctrine of creation, the doctrine of the Father of Jesus Christ creating humanity for the sake of Jesus Christ; through Him by the power of the Holy Spirit. There is a subtle but drastically important change of thought between Barth's doctrine of creation and the common, general doctrines of creation found elsewhere. These have often passed as Christian doctrines, but in reality, these have more in common with pagan doctrines of creation than with Jesus Christ as the beginning of God's ways and works. Barth does not see creation as merely moving *towards* Christ, but as moving *from* Christ and *toward* Christ and *with* Christ from first to last as the Alpha and Omega of all things. This excludes the notion of His reconciling work of grace as a reactionary work. God had this work in mind all along.

The first quote from Barth above shows this distinction perhaps the clearest. For Barth, it is not Adam and *then* Christ, it is *Christ* and then Adam. Jesus Christ does not assume human flesh within *Adam's* world, Adam comes into being within *Christ's* world. The incarnation and the reconciliation of the world with God in Jesus Christ, the person and the work, do not take place as a reaction to Adam, but as God's eternal will for humanity. Accordingly, human beings, even in their sin, are never *neutral* before God but are always under the grace of God. Kathryn Tanner writes:

> God's decision to be for us in Jesus is not a reaction to previous events in the history of God's relations with us, but has a reality in its own right preceding the whole of that history. What is first in God's intention and what spurs God's relation with us from the very beginning—to be the loving Father of us all in Jesus Christ—comes last in execution. Therefore the history of God's relations with us, like the Bible, has to be read from back to front and only on that basis from the front in anticipation of the end.

> — THE CAMBRIDGE COMPANION TO KARL BARTH, 114

In other words, creation begins with its goal in mind, with God's becoming man in Jesus Christ as the presupposition of creation and not as an afterthought to God's act in creating. We read history rightly when we read from last to first, from Christ to Adam, *not* from Adam to Christ. Creation is not a general event which then includes the covenant of grace as an afterthought; creation follows the covenant of grace, proceeding *after* God's decision to become a man for us in Jesus Christ and to suffer our sin and take our place as sinners on the cross. In short, God's will for reconciliation precedes the event of creation. Before the world was made, and even before the fall, God planned to reconcile the world to Godself so that we might be the objects of God's love.

Creation has its basis in the Word of God, in Jesus Christ, and in *this* Word alone. There is no other basis for creation. In this sense, Barth's doctrine of creation is a rejection of natural theology. Rather than forming a doctrine of creation by philosophically speculating God as the "first cause" of the world, Barth begins with the Word of God in Jesus Christ as the fulfillment of the covenant of grace and therefore as the internal basis of creation. A Christian cosmology cannot begin speculatively with a general creator God, but instead, it must begin concretely with Jesus Christ through whom and for whom the world and human beings were made.

There is one final consideration to be made before summarizing Barth's doctrine of creation in *CD* III. That is, how does the covenant of grace compare to what is known as "covenant theology" (or sometimes "federal theology")?

Covenant theology essentially imagines that God has made several covenants (plural) with select communities, which were all eventually broken until the final "new" covenant of grace was formed in Jesus Christ. Covenant theology divides the Old Testament into various periods of overarching covenants, such as the Adamic, Noahic, Abrahamic, Mosaic, and Davidic covenants. However, you can see how this sort of thinking is in line with a *reactionary* doctrine of creation and reconciliation. Barth is therefore diametrically opposed to it from the start. Instead, Barth argues that there is only *one* covenant, the covenant of grace, which underlies the whole history of creation, and therefore not a multitude of covenants between God and humanity. The covenant may take on different forms, but it is always the one covenant will of God to be gracious and to reconcile the world in Jesus Christ.

Instead of speculatively imagining that God first hoped humanity would fulfill the law and live in God's covenant by their own strength, Barth argues that God had always planned to fulfill and uphold the covenant in the person and work of Jesus Christ. God's covenant was and is forever the covenant of grace; it is not first a covenant of works and then a reactionary covenant of grace. There is *one* covenant, the fulfilled covenant in the person of Jesus Christ for our sakes as both God towards humanity and a human towards God.

We won't discuss the merits of this or how Barth refutes covenant theology, but it's worth making this clear from the start. When Barth talks about the covenant, he means God's *one* covenant of grace, the only covenant between God and humanity. This has nothing to do with the false duality inherent to covenant theology, which ultimately posits various covenant wills in God. For Barth, Jesus Christ and the covenant of grace established in Him is alone the underlying reality behind creation.

HUMANITY AND EVIL IN THE LIGHT OF JESUS CHRIST

Since Jesus Christ and the covenant fulfilled in Him precedes creation and is not a reaction in creation, Barth develops a doctrine of humanity, providence, evil, and of special ethics, all in the light of Jesus Christ. We'll briefly summarize Barth's doctrine of creation from what remains in *CD* III.

In *CD* III/2, we come to understand human beings as God's creature, determined to be God's covenant-partner, comprising of a soul and body ("embodied soul and besouled body") within the limits of time. Only in and through Jesus Christ is humanity known as such, since Jesus Christ is the true man for God, the true man for other human beings, the whole person, and the Lord of time.

From this (*CD* III/3), Barth moves onto the doctrine of providence, as God's Fatherly preserving, accompanying, and ruling creation as its Lord. Notably, this is where Barth develops a doctrine of "nothingness" or "nihility" (as Robert W. Jenson preferred to translate it). Jenson summarizes this doctrine, writing:

> Nihility has existence as a by-product of God's eternal decision of grace, of His decision to reconcile fallen man to Himself. It exists only as the necessary object of its own overcoming, and it is this overthrow which is positively willed by God.

— ALPHA AND OMEGA, 36

Barth's doctrine of nothingness is best understood in the light of Christ's overcoming of it on the cross, in the light of the crucifixion. In this regard, Barth writes:

> In plain and precise terms, the answer is that nothingness is the 'reality' on whose account (i.e., against which) God Himself willed to become a creature in the creaturely world, yielding and subjecting Himself to it in Jesus Christ in order to overcome it.

— CD III/3, 305

And Barth further defines nothingness, writing:

> Nothingness is that which God does not will. It lives only by the fact that it is that which God does not will. But it does live by this fact. For not only what God wills, but what He does not will, is potent, and must have a real correspondence.

— CD III/3, 352

Nothingness is what God has overcome in Jesus Christ, what He is the Victor over, and therefore it *was* and no longer *is*. Its very being is in its being defeated and overcome by Jesus Christ. Nothingness is Barth's doctrine of sin and evil. It is the disorder that God did not will, the shadow of God's positive determination to love the creature and be their Lord. As such, it is the "ontological impossibility" of creation. Nothingness has no basis in God and therefore no ontological reality, yet it *is,* or more precisely, *was* since it exists only as that which God has overcome.

Following nothingness, Barth concludes *CD* III/3 with the Kingdom of Heaven, which includes Barth's angelology. And finally, Barth concludes the doctrine of creation with the command of God, with a special ethics, in *CD* III/4. This volume follows the same pattern as *CD* III/2, with human beings in their freedom for God, for each other, for life, and in the limitation of time.

The key idea behind all of this has already been preeminently established in III/1. Creation follows the covenant and therefore an understanding of humanity, providence, nothingness, and ethics must all be worked out in the light of that covenant, namely, in the light of Jesus Christ. Barth continually reminds us that we are not dealing with a general God preeminently established in our minds before examining the Scriptures; the only truly Christian doctrine of creation begins with the God and Father of Jesus Christ as the Creator. It is *this* God and not another who must be the subject of our study of creation. In this sense, Barth presents a thoroughly *Christian* doctrine, against the semi-pagan doctrines about a general, "first cause" creator.

CREATION AS BENEFIT

In creation, God says Yes to us and not No. Creation, as such, is *benefit.* It is for our good, corresponding to the goodwill of the Creator. This notion is a compelling aspect of Barth's doctrine of creation, and it summarizes well many of the ideas we've covered so far. Accordingly, we'll end this chapter with an extended quotation on creation as benefit:

> God the creator did not say No, nor Yes and No, but Yes to what He created. There is, of course, a divine No as well: the necessary rejection of everything which by His own nature God cannot be; and consequently the necessary rejection of everything which again by His own nature God cannot will and create, and cannot even tolerate as a reality distinct from Himself. [...] Creation has to do with this non-real element [with nothingness] only in so far as it consists inevitably in its exclusion. Creation as such is not rejection, but election and acceptance. It is God's positing in accordance with His nature of a reality which is distinct from

Him but willed by Him. As a work of God turned outwards it participates in the right, dignity and goodness of this Yes in which He is God by Himself. As God in creation manifests His inner being outwardly, as in supreme faithfulness and not unfaithfulness to Himself He says Yes not only to Himself but also to another, creation is divine benefit. For it is the essence of all divine being and therefore all true benefit that in supreme faithfulness to Himself God rejoices in another which as such has not shared in the divine being; that He honours and approves this other within the limits of its distinct being. Creation is benefit because it takes place according to God's beneficence, and therefore according to the supreme law of all benevolence and *bene esse* [well being]. Creation is blessing because it has unchangeably the character of an action in which the divine joy, honour and affirmation are turned towards another. [...]

The Christian apprehension of creation requires and involves the principle that creation is benefit. It shows us God's good-pleasure as the root, the foundation and the end of divine creation. It suggests the peace with which God separated and protected what He truly willed from what He did not will, and therefore from the unreal. It implies that God Himself, in and with the beginning of all things, decided for His creation and made Himself the responsible Guarantor of it. Creation, as it is known by the Christian, is benefit.

— CD III/1, 330-2

SIGNIFICANCE: Barth's doctrine of creation re-affirms the Yes of God to the creature in Jesus Christ. The classic philosophical question, "Why is there something rather than nothing?", is answered by God's love for humanity. Creation is *benefit*; it is our good. God is neither hostile or neutral towards us, but before the beginning of all things, God determined to be *God for us*.

Furthermore, Barth's doctrine of creation is a truly *Christian* doctrine in the sense that he refocuses our attention on the person of Jesus Christ as the beginning of God's ways and works. Rather than imagining a world which comes into being *apart* from Jesus Christ, or which contains Jesus

Christ as an *afterthought,* Barth makes Christ's person and work central. Even before the foundations of the world, God willed to be a man for our sakes, to reconcile and redeem the world in the Son. We misunderstand the life and death of Jesus Christ if we imagine these taking place in the light of human sin, as a reactionary event to that sin, rather than as an event God willed from before all time.

SIDEBAR: NON-HISTORICAL HISTORY

Barth makes a careful distinction between historical history and non-historical history in *CD* III. Historical history is history perceivable and comprehensible to human beings. It is the kind of history we know in history books, such as the historical report of a baseball game, the results of an election, or World War II. This history is historical in the sense that human beings can perceive it and comprehend it *by themselves* as an event like all other events in time.

Non-historical history, however, is the kind of history human beings cannot perceive or comprehend in themselves, the history which does not compare with any other similar event in time. Two examples of this non-historical history are the creation of the world and the resurrection of Jesus Christ. Both events are non-historical in the sense that no human being was present to perceive them, but also that they would not be comprehensible or perceivable in and of themselves even if someone was present for them. These sorts of events indeed *happened* but they are not under the control of human categorization, and therefore they are not historical in the historical sense that one might perceive them through history. They are characterized by the in-breaking of God's grace. A historian could not adequately perceive or record these events, and therefore they are events of non-historical history. This distinction protects the uniqueness of these events as *God's* work in history, as *miraculous* events.

Barth explains this distinction in an insightful passage from the doctrine of creation (*CD* III/1):

> But history which we cannot see and comprehend is not history in the historicist sense. This history, i.e., the history which is accessible to man because it is visible and perceptible to him and can be comprehended as history, is from the objective standpoint creaturely history in the content of other creaturely history, as an event prior to which and side by side with which there are other events of the same basic type with which it can be compared and integrated. [...] But it is just this content that the history of creation lacks. Its only content is God the Creator. For this reason it is not history in the historicist sense, and there can be no history of it. For this reason it is 'non-historical' history, and it can be the subject only of a 'non-historical' history. [...] This is particularly the case where history assumes the character of miracle. It is most apparent at the centre of the history of the covenant of grace—in the resurrection of Jesus Christ. What does it really mean to see and grasp a real miracle? What does it mean to perceive and establish a resurrection from the dead? In this case the historical element in the event seems almost to have disappeared and the 'non-historical' to have taken the upper hand. Even the human account of it, the description of the event, seems necessarily to have to burst through the framework of historical relation. [...] For what *could* actually be perceptible and comprehensible and therefore 'historical' in this story?
>
> — CD III/1, 78-9

Why are we discussing this here? It is necessary to clarify the way Barth navigates the event of the resurrection of Jesus Christ and the creation of the world. Some have said that Barth *denies* the bodily resurrection of Christ, but nothing could be further from the truth. Barth insists this event did *happen*, and in fact, the resurrection is central to his entire theology. But Barth is not interested in making this event an occurrence that human perception can *control* and therefore *master*. It is *God's* miraculous raising of Jesus Christ by the power of the Spirit, and that means it is not fundamentally a *human* event. It is a miracle of grace. It is, therefore, a historical event not in the sense that it is a story accessible to human history, like the sinking of the Titanic or the signing of the Declaration of Independence. It is an event of non-historical history, that is, of God's Kingdom come, of God's will be done on earth as it is in heaven. The resurrection is thus not something we might discover if we were to investigate it historically (as some have attempted) since it is known to us only by faith in God's revelation, as God makes Godself known as the God who raises the dead.

For Barth, this distinction reaffirms his rejection of natural theology. We cannot attain a natural knowledge of God as the God who resurrected Jesus Christ any more than we can achieve natural knowledge of God as the Father and Creator of the world. Both are a confession of faith. These are not naturally obtainable facts through historical inquiry, but confessions. This retains God's freedom over and against our ability to perceive these events. The God who raises the dead makes Godself known as such only by self-revelation. As with God's revelation of Godself—that we cannot know God unless God reveals God through Godself—so it is true that we cannot know the *works* of God unless God likewise reveals them through Godself.

To be clear, this doesn't mean Barth turns the resurrection and creation events into merely "faith events" which have no actualization in history. Barth does not deny that Jesus Christ was raised bodily in Jerusalem sometime around 30AD, nor does he deny the empty tomb. Instead, Barth insists upon stressing the *uniqueness* of these events, not only in their character as miracles but also in our ability to know them. We could not know the events of creation or Christ's resurrection if God had not first revealed these things to us. Both events are therefore outside of our perception and comprehension. They are events of "non-historical" history.

Let us be clear: Karl Barth confesses, with the whole Church and the Apostles' Creed, that on the third day Jesus Christ rose again bodily from the grave. In *CD* III/2, Barth strongly insists we must believe in the resurrection:

> Either we believe with the New Testament in the risen Jesus Christ, or we do not believe in Him at all. [...] While we could

imagine a New Testament containing only the history of Easter and its message, we could not possibly imagine a New Testament without it. ...Everything else in the New Testament contains and presupposes the resurrection. It is the key to the whole.

— CD III/2, 443

There should be no doubt: Karl Barth affirms the resurrection. Although, like many things in Barth's theology, he is so carefully nuanced and thoroughly exhaustive, almost to a fault, that he risks being misunderstood by those who gloss over his logic and jump straight to his conclusions. Claiming that Barth denies the resurrection is a sure sign of missing the point, however, and it means failing to follow Barth's logic carefully and with the attention it deserves.

Sermon: witnessed, not described

In a sermon to prisoners at Basel, Barth follows this same pattern we've discussed. He affirms the resurrection as an event which *truly* happened, but at once he carefully describes it as an event incomprehensible to human means of historical investigation. It is an event that actually happened in history, but it is not an event we can reach by our own efforts; it is only made known to us by grace through faith.

The raising of Jesus was utterly and completely the work of God; as such it was indeed well done but also quite incomprehensible. Even at the time, it could only be recognized, acknowledge, attested and declared that such a thing had taken place. 'Jesus Christ is risen' is how one Christian greets another today [Easter] in Russia, to which then the other answers: 'He is risen indeed!' But this is the point: that is not describing, it is witnessing and declaring. ... This man who earlier had died was now alive in the way that God is alive and was alive in God's power, living directly by him and with him and therefore undying, immortal and incorruptible. It was in this way that Jesus came to his disciples that day. That much could be clearly told, however stammeringly. And in this narrative there was and is attested and declared, at the same time and right to this day, something that could not and cannot be described in words: the resurrection of Jesus.

— CALL FOR GOD, 118-9

We are called to bear *witness* to the resurrection, to the risen Jesus Christ, but we cannot attempt to describe it because it is beyond human words. That is Barth's point in making the distinction between non-historical history and historical history.

SERMON: THE FEAR OF THE LORD

Barth makes a necessary clarification on the "fear of the Lord" which is "the beginning of wisdom." The verses before this famous phrase in Psalm 110 focus on the goodness of God. These verses give thanks to God for God's wonderful works, for the fact that God is gracious and merciful and that God is ever mindful of the covenant. This is the context of the Biblical saying that the fear of the Lord is the beginning of wisdom. Unfortunately, many take that one sentence and declare it from the rooftops without first considering its context, which is a meditation on the goodness, faithfulness, and gracefulness of the creator God.

In this regard, Barth comments:

> This is the [true] fear of the Lord: it is born, it is given as soon as man discovers that God is *this* God and does *these* things of which the psalm speaks. It is nothing short of a discovery when a man is suddenly confronted with this reality. It is not unlike the experience of Columbus who, sailing out for India, suddenly hit upon the continent of America. *This* I did not know. *This* nobody ever told me. *This* I could never have found out by myself—that God is *this* God, that God does *these* things. [...] When the right fear of the Lord takes possession of our hearts, we are both lost in amazement and struck by awe, even terror. For we discover that

God, since the beginning of time, has not hated or threatened you and me, but has loved and chosen us, has made a covenant with us, has been our helper long before we knew it and will continue this relationship. The fear of the Lord springs from the discovery that the high and eternal God gave his beloved son for us, for you and me, taking upon himself our sin and our misery; he made his son, our Lord Jesus Christ, to be our brother, for whose sake we may call God our Father and ourselves his children. The fear of the Lord springs from the discovery that I did not merit this gift, that it has been given to me by the pure and free goodness of God, in spite of all I deserved. The fear of the Lord springs from the discovery that this is the true relationship between God and me—that I had totally ignored it—that I had perhaps heard it once from afar, only to forget it again and to live as if it were not true and none of my concern.

— Deliverance to the Captives, 133

God was and willed all these things before the foundations of the world. That is Barth's point in discussing the doctrine of creation as the external basis of the covenant. Creation is the joyful overflowing act of *this* God who wills to be *our God* and therefore to do *these things* for our salvation unto fellowship with Godself.

We come into the world and imagine that it is a neutral world or a hostile world, but the world God has made is neither hostile or indifferent. It is *affirmative*. Creation is the *Yes* of the creator, the *Yes* for fellowship and life and joy.

7

RECONCILIATION

SUMMARY: Reconciliation *is* Jesus Christ, God with us: the Son of God in humiliation, the Judge judged in our place; the Son of Man in exaltation, the Royal Man; the God-man and Mediator, the Victor. Barth presents reconciliation as the objective fact of our existence in Him, not as an opportunity we submit to or obtain abstractly apart from Jesus Christ. It is *the* event of all history, the culmination of God's primal will, the fulfillment of the covenant. Barth developed this doctrine in the terms of traditional Christology, as Jesus Christ is true God, true man, the God-man.

IN BARTH'S OWN WORDS:

The content of the doctrine of reconciliation is the knowledge of *Jesus Christ* who is 1. the true God, namely the God who humbles himself and thus brings reconciliation; 2. the true man who is exalted by God and thus reconciled to him, and 3. in the unity of the two is the guarantor and witness to our reconciliation. This threefold knowledge of Jesus Christ includes knowledge of man's *sin:* 1. his arrogance, 2. his sloth, 3. his lies—the knowledge of the event in which the reconciliation *takes place:* 1. his justification, 2. his sanctification, 3. his vocation—and the knowledge of the work of the Holy Spirit in 1. gathering together, 2.

building up, and 3. sending the community, and of the being of
Christians in Jesus Christ 1. in faith, 2. in love and 3. in hope.

— CD IV/1, 79; JOHN BOWDEN TRANS., QUOTED IN
BUSCH, 378

Jesus Christ is the atonement. But that means that He is the maintaining
and accomplishing and fulfilling of the divine covenant as executed by
God Himself.

— CD IV/1, 122

SECONDARY QUOTES:

The person of Christ *is* his saving work, so that an adequately articulated
Christology will also be a theology of salvation.

— COLIN GUNTON: "SALVATION" CAMBRIDGE
COMPANION, 144

According to Barth, the key to the doctrine of the atonement is that the
death and resurrection of Jesus Christ was an event in the life of God.
[...] God brought the resources of his own being and life as the triune
God in the fullness of the divine perfections to bear upon our fallen
condition so as to save us, bringing us to fellowship with himself. [...]
That God was in Christ, and in this specific way reconciling all things to
himself, is the decisive and pre-eminent foundation for understanding
the work of Jesus Christ.

— ADAM J. JOHNSON: GOD'S BEING IN RECONCILIATION,
22

FIVE POINTS OF EMPHASIS

Our first quotation is from Barth's summary thesis in §58, "The Doctrine
of Reconciliation (Survey)" in *CD* IV/1. It is helpful that Barth first establishes a full outline of his doctrine of reconciliation because here Barth is

perhaps the most creative. He constructs what has sometimes been called a "mini-dogmatics" (at nearly 3,000 pages). The structure of the doctrine of reconciliation from *CD* IV is nothing short of a stroke of genius, for several reasons. There are five major points of emphasis that led Barth to structure this volume the way he did; we'll briefly explore each of these before discussing the doctrine.

The first point of emphasis is Barth's refusal to develop a doctrine of soteriology (salvation) apart from Christology (Jesus Christ), which explains the structure of the volumes which make up *CD* IV. Barth focuses on the person of Jesus Christ as true God, true man, and true God-man; and he arranges the doctrine of reconciliation around each as the true God *humbled* (IV/1), the true man *exalted* (IV/2), and the true God-man as mediator, witness, and guarantee of reconciliation (IV/3).

The second point of emphasis is Barth's refusal to treat the person and work of Jesus Christ separately. We see this present already in the previous refusal to separate soteriology and Christology. When Christology and soteriology are treated separately, the significance of Christ's work is ultimately separated from the significance of the person of Christ; there is emphasized a "for me" of Christ's work but not also a "for me" of the *person* of Christ. Barth refused to speak in this way and instead emphasized the fact that the person and the work are inseparable. "Jesus Christ is the atonement." This does not dissolve His person into His work or vice versa, but it refuses to treat them separately.

The third point of emphasis is Barth's refusal to treat sin independently, as an isolated doctrine apart from Jesus Christ and its overcoming in Him. There is no independent knowledge of sin, Barth argues, apart from the revelation of God's triumph over sin in Jesus Christ. Sin is known only in the light of its defeat in God's humiliation, exaltation, and guarantee. Thus Barth does not develop a doctrine of sin until *after* the doctrine of Christ's person and work has been explained. Therefore sin is our pride (our arrogance) overcome by Christ's humiliation as true God (IV/1), it is our sloth overcome by Christ's exaltation as true man (IV/2), and it is our falsehood (our lies) overcome by Christ as true witness and mediator (IV/3).

The fourth point of emphasis is Barth's refusal to make independently central either justification, sanctification, or vocation; he focuses instead on all three aspects in the doctrine of reconciliation. Lutheranism tends to make justification the central issue, pietism tends to make sanctification the central issue, and Anglicanism tends to make vocation the central issue. Barth embraces all three and stresses their equal importance. He acts therefore as a true *ecumenical* theologian.

The fifth and final point of emphasis is Barth's refusal to present an independent doctrine of the Holy Spirit. He includes it as an integral aspect of the doctrine of reconciliation. The Holy Spirit as the power of Jesus Christ is the "subjective realization" of reconciliation accomplished in Him, and therefore Barth includes in the doctrine of the Holy Spirit the doctrine of the Church gathered (IV/1), built up (IV/2), and sent out (IV/3) in the Holy Spirit; and within the community the individual is awakened to faith (IV/1), quickened to love (IV/2), and enlightened to hope (IV/3) in the Holy Spirit.

These five points of emphasis cause the structure of the doctrine of reconciliation to take its particular shape. Each emphasis is brilliant in its own right but put them all together, and you have a work of pure genius. In my opinion, this is Barth's greatest legacy as a theologian, and it is why I will recommend later on a reading of volume IV as an introductory way to read the whole of Barth's theology.

But consider just one of the practical implications of this. For example, imagine the profound implications of applying Barth's doctrine of sin. How often today is sin treated independently of Jesus Christ as if to give sin equal weight against Him? How might our preaching and teaching of the gospel and ethics, not to mention our pastoral concerns, be rethought in the light of this refusal to speak of sin independent of its overcoming in Jesus Christ? This is just one of the insights that have far-reaching implications in this volume. We won't, unfortunately, have the time to dive into the depths of each issue at hand, but instead, a general outline will be presented. But the subtle radicalism of this doctrine shouldn't be glossed over. Barth has important, far-reaching things to teach the Church in this volume.

We'll first begin our outline with Jesus Christ as God humbled, man exalted, and as reconciliation guaranteed. Second, with human sin as pride, sloth, and falsehood. Third, with justification, sanctification, and vocation. And finally, with the Holy Spirit upbuilding, gathering, and sending the Church; and awakening faith, quickening love, and enlightening hope in the individual.

Two Further Considerations

Before diving into the content of Barth's doctrine of reconciliation, I want to take a step back and look at two further considerations which give a more general perspective on Barth's doctrine.

The first general consideration is clearly seen in the original, alternative title Barth had in mind for this volume. Barth at one point entertained the idea of calling it "the doctrine of the covenant," but decided to keep with the more traditional title, "the doctrine of reconciliation" (Busch, 377). Why is this significant? Plainly, because it shows how essential the covenant is to the whole of Barth's thought on reconciliation. We should read his doctrine of reconciliation in the light of what we've already discussed in the doctrine of creation, with the covenant being the internal basis of creation and grace as the beginning of all God's ways and works. Reconciliation is the fulfillment of God's covenant will, the covenant of grace, which precedes creation itself.

Jesus Christ is the fulfillment of the covenant both in the faithfulness of God towards humanity and the faithfulness of humanity towards God. He fulfilled both sides of the covenant in Himself, both as God to humanity and a human to God. The fulfillment of the covenant in Jesus Christ was central for Barth as he worked out the whole doctrine.

The second general consideration is to make note of the two Scriptures Barth considered to be useful summaries of the doctrine of reconciliation. These are John 3:16 and 2 Corinthians 5:19: "God so loved the world that He gave his only begotten Son," and "God was in Christ, reconciling the world to Himself." These two passages are essential for Barth's doctrine of reconciliation (see *CD* IV/1, 70-8). Barth takes these seriously enough to say already in *CD* II/2, "Dogmatics has no more exalted or profound word—essentially, indeed, it has no other word— than this: that God was in Christ reconciling the world unto Himself" (88).

The emphasis in both of these Scriptures is on the *God* who loved and the *God* who was in Christ. In this sense, Barth understands reconciliation as God bearing the full weight of God's *being* upon our sinful humanity, giving Godself over to our condition without giving up Godself. In fact, Barth goes so far as to say God *hazards* God's very existence for our sakes. This is the astounding reality behind these words that God so loved and therefore *gave,* that *God* was in Christ. The importance here is to note that, for Barth, the work of reconciliation is not accomplished by some divine tool; the humanity of Jesus Christ was not a piece of duct tape God used to patch up a leaky faucet. Jesus Christ is God in Godself giving Godself over to our existence, gifting *Godself* for our sake, for our salvation—all the while without giving *up* Godself. Thus Barth emphasizes the atonement accomplished and the covenant fulfilled only *in Christ,* in Jesus Christ who is God humbled to our existence, the God of humanity.

These two general considerations help us frame the picture we must now paint of Barth's doctrine of reconciliation.

1. Jesus Christ is God humbled, man exalted, RECONCILIATION WITNESSED AND MEDIATED

The first part of the doctrine of reconciliation focuses on Jesus Christ as true God, true man, and true God-man. Barth stresses that these so-called states of Christ as humbled and exalted are not static but dynamic states. God in Christ is not here humbled and there exalted, but *at once* and in union with Jesus Christ humbled and exalted as true God and true man.

(IV/1) That God comes to us in humiliation relates to the priestly office of Jesus Christ. Jesus Christ is true God who has taken up our cause as His own, who has become a man in humiliation. He is the Lord as a servant. This is not outside of God's nature as God but reveals that God is as high and exalted as He is lowly and humbled. It does not contradict God's being as God to become humbled and take up our cause and even suffer our death, but this has been revealed about God in Jesus Christ. Barth places this under the heading "The Obedience of the Son of God" (§59), which includes sub-sections on 1) "The Way of the Son of God into the Far Country," 2) "The Judge Judged in our Place," and 3) "The Verdict of the Father." Jesus Christ takes our place as the transgressor, going in obedience into the "Far Country" of our humanity, and here Christ displaces us as a false judge (pretending we can judge ourselves) and acts as the True Judge who is Judged in our place. Christ's death is the end of the sinner, of the old nature, and of the old creation. The third sub-section on "The Verdict of the Father" deals with the resurrection and acts as a kind of transitional section, essentially asking the question of how this event which takes place in Jesus Christ so long ago can have any relevance for us today. For this, Barth points to the resurrection.

(IV/2) That mankind is exalted to God relates to the kingly office of Jesus Christ. Jesus Christ is not only the Son of God humbled, but at once He is the Son of Man exalted to God. He is the servant as Lord. Barth places this under the heading, "The Exaltation of the Son of Man" (§64), which includes sub-sections on 1) "The Homecoming of the Son of Man," 2) "The Royal Man," and 3) "The Direction of the Son." Jesus Christ as the true man exalts humanity in Him to participation in the life of God, to fellowship with God, and therefore reconciliation takes place in this exaltation. "God becomes man in order that man may—not become God, but come to God" (*CD* IV/2, 106). Barth develops a robust Christology here as he deals with the humanity of Jesus Christ. He hopes to do in a different way what was done already in the first volume as God humbled in Jesus Christ: to explain reconciliation from this other direction, from Jesus Christ as true man exalted, as the Royal Man. In this sub-section, Barth pays special attention to the actions (or miracles) of Jesus, as this Royal Man. In the third sub-section on the "Direction of the Son," Barth again engages in a transitionary discussion, pointing to the resurrection.

(IV/3) That God and man are one in Jesus Christ relates to the prophetic office of Jesus Christ. Jesus Christ is Victor and the true witness of reconciliation. As reconciliation takes place in Him, this event at once *reveals* itself in Him. It is not a mute occurrence but speaks. Barth places this under the heading, "The Glory of the Mediator" (§69). This includes sub-sections on 1) "The Light of Life," 2) "Jesus is Victor," and 3) "The Promise of the Spirit." In Jesus Christ the mediator we hear Gods "active and superior" Yes to humanity, to the world. This is the fulfillment of God's eternal election, God's determination to say Yes to humanity in Jesus Christ, to be our God and for us to be God's people. Reconciliation proclaims itself. The material content of reconciliation has been covered in *CD* IV/1-2, but here in *CD* IV/3 Barth is concerned with the knowledge of reconciliation as it proclaims itself in Him. As the Light of Life Jesus Christ speaks for Himself, as His own true witness. Here Barth deals again with the doctrine of revelation in quite a unique and brilliant way, though not a totally different way than what is found in *CD* I and II. He also presents a fascinating discussion of "secular parables" of the kingdom.

Turning to the covenant, that Jesus is Victor means that God has fulfilled this covenant. "[Jesus Christ] is present as the Victor from the very outset. He is life; in Him the covenant is fulfilled; in Him reconciliation is effected" (*CD* IV/3.1, 173). In the final sub-section, Barth again points to the resurrection as a transitionary discussion, here in terms of the Promise of the Spirit, asking again how all this can have its effect on us today.

2. Sin in the light of Jesus Christ as pride, sloth, and falsehood

Barth develops a doctrine of sin in the light of Christ's overcoming of it, and therefore his considerations regarding humanity's sin directly correspond to the work of Christ in its preceding section.

(IV/1) First, sin is understood in the light of the obedience of Jesus Christ, God humbled. Barth writes:

> [W]e maintain the simple thesis that only when we know Jesus Christ do we really know that man is the man of sin, and what sin is, and what it means for man.
>
> — CD IV/1, 389

In the light of God's humiliation, the sinner overcome in Him is revealed to be the prideful individual. Jesus Christ is God in our flesh, in our sinful pride we want to be God. Jesus Christ is the Lord as a servant, in our sinful pride we want to be the lord. Jesus Christ is the Judge judged in our place, in our sinful pride we desire to be our own judge. Jesus Christ suffers and dies helpless and alone, relying only on His Father for help, and in our sinful pride, we in true helplessness are under the illusion of self-help. This is our pride. After pride comes the fall. But Barth is quick here to point out that, "Man has not fallen lower than the depth to which God humbled Himself for him in Jesus Christ" (*CD* IV/1, 481). But we have fallen, and the radical depths of our fall are revealed in Christ's coming to us in humiliation.

(IV/2) Second, sin is understood in the light of the lordship of the Son of Man, man exalted. Again Barth stresses the fact that we can only know the sinner who has been overcome in Jesus Christ in the light of that overcoming, and not before, not abstractly. There is no independent doctrine of sin, but only that which is revealed in Jesus Christ's work of reconciliation. In the light of the exaltation of man to God in Jesus Christ, the sinner overcome in Him is revealed to be the slothful individual. This is the stupidity of the sinner unwilling to know God, the inhumanity of the sinner who wills to be without their fellow-man, the dissipation or disorder of the sinner at odds with their own nature as a human being, and the anxiety of the sinner in the face of their limitation. This is our sloth. Sloth breeds misery, ending in the totality of human suffering. But Jesus Christ has taken up our suffering as His own, He has suffered with us, and by suffering with us, He has taken us home and healed us by reconciling us to Godself. Therefore even our misery is not too great for Jesus Christ to meet us there and heal us. But it is great, and the depth of our misery is unveiled by God's coming to us in this way.

(IV/3) Third, sin is understood in the light of the true witness, the God-man and mediator. As before, the nature of the sin of the sinner is known in the light of Christ's overcoming it. But just as here we are dealing with the *revelation* of reconciliation, and not with its material content, so we are not dealing with the works of the sinner, but with the *word* of the sinner. Thus we are confronted with the fact that the sin of the sinner is their falsehood. The sinner lies. The truth of God encounters us in Jesus Christ as He proclaims reconciliation; but the sinner stands in untruth, attempting an impossible freedom from God's Word of reconciliation in Jesus Christ. In this sense, the sin of the sinner is the attempt to hide from the truth of their reconciliation and to live in falsehood and untruth. And this leads to the condemnation of the sinner. The gospel does not condemn humanity. It is God's Yes not God's No. But the sinner who lives in falsehood brings condemnation upon themselves by refusing to live in the truth. This "no" of the sinner to grace is nonsensical since sin defies understanding. "What he [the sinner] chooses and draws down upon himself with his falsehood is his condemnation" (*CD* IV/3.1, 462). This is the nonsensical rejection of grace, the "Well, I'll be damned!" of the sinner who chooses to live in stubborn untruth. But while their condemnation may finally hold out to the end, and the sinner may suffer damnation, there is still hope for every sinner because their untruth is not beyond the light of revelation. Barth presents at the very end of this section an appeal to the freedom of God as the final word on the question of universalism. Ultimately, only God will one day answer the question. Until then, we take sin seriously with hope in the possibility of final and total redemption.

3. THE EVENT OF RECONCILIATION TAKES PLACE IN HUMANITY'S JUSTIFICATION, SANCTIFICATION, AND VOCATION

The sinner is overcome. This sinner is justified, sanctified, and called to a vocation in Jesus Christ. This sinner becomes the new creature, the saint. Here Barth presents a common paradox. The human being is no longer the sinner because Christ has overcome and put to death this sinner, but at one time we indeed were this individual. We *are* now and are still *becoming* the new creation established in Christ's resurrection, but we are not yet this new creation. We are individuals on the way between Good Friday and Easter Sunday. We are not what we were, but we are not yet what we are becoming. It's in this context that Barth discusses the doctrines of justification, sanctification, and vocation. These are first of all *God's* justification, sanctification, and vocation, and then only in Him do they become ours. Jesus Christ Himself *is* the justification, sanctification, and calling of humanity, and only in Him are we justified, sanctified, and called. The point here is to take these events out of our hands and to understand them only in relation to Jesus Christ.

(IV/1) Justification is God's "right" established in the death of Jesus Christ and proclaimed in His resurrection. God justifies Godself. God justifies Godself against the sinful wrong done by human beings. Justification is promised to humanity in Jesus Christ, yet it is at once hidden in Him and thereby revealed only in Him. Thus it cannot be received or achieved by our efforts, but by grace alone. We are therefore called by justification to faith, to the acknowledgment, appropriation, and application of our justification in Him. We are justified in Him by grace through faith.

(IV/2) Sanctification is the creation of a new form of existence, of the new creation, posited in Jesus Christ's resurrection. This new existence is that of a faithful covenant-partner with God. Sanctification, therefore, rests on justification. If justification is the "I will be your God" of reconciliation—God's taking up our cause as God's own, establishing our justification in Godself—then sanctification is the "you shall be my people."

This includes the fact that we are made holy and righteous *in Jesus Christ,* who is our sanctification. "As we are not asked to justify ourselves, we are not asked to sanctify ourselves" (*CD* IV/2, 517). Therefore, we have to do here with an act of God's grace towards us. In this connection, Barth reflects on the call of discipleship, of our awakening to conversion, of the praise of works (which deals with the *false* notion that faith and works are at odds with one another), and finally on the dignity of the cross and our part in bearing it. We are sanctified in Him by grace through faith.

(IV/3) Vocation is God's calling, God's witness to reconciliation in Jesus Christ, awakening human beings to the knowledge of the truth, to receive a new standing as Christians participating in fellowship with God acting as themselves witnesses to the truth. The Christian is not a Christian for their own end, but for the sake of being His witnesses. Just as in the prior sections, when the first two aspects dealt with the material content of the doctrine, this third section likewise deals with the revelation of that material content. The Christian is called to an active knowledge of the truth, and therefore they are made responsible for it by becoming witnesses to Jesus Christ. Here Barth discusses the event and the goal of the Christian's vocation, followed by a discussion on the Christian as a witness, the Christian in affliction, and the liberation of the Christian. We are called in Him by grace through faith.

4. The Holy Spirit as the power of Jesus Christ is the subjective realization of reconciliation in the Church and the individual

It is an error to say Barth has no place for the subjective element in his theology, as if there is no *effect* of Jesus Christ upon humanity. That is what we've come to consider here. In this final section Barth addresses the doctrine of the Holy Spirit as the *subjective realization* of reconciliation, first in the Church as the community of the Holy Spirit, and second in the individual by the Holy Spirit.

(IV/1) In the community, the Holy Spirit is the "awakening" power of God by whom Jesus Christ forms and renews His body. The Church is therefore called the "earthly-historical" form of the existence of Jesus Christ. This is the gathering of the community, which is the "provisional representation of the whole world of humanity justified in Him." The

Holy Spirit awakens the community, gathering the community as the body of Jesus Christ. This community is the One, Holy, Apostolic Church. Barth reflects on the being of the community as Christ's earthly-historical existence, and the time of the community in between the resurrection and final consummation.

In the individual, the Holy Spirit is the awakening power of God through whom Jesus Christ summons the individual to faith in Him, through whom He summons the individual within the community to acknowledge and know and confess Jesus Christ as Lord, and thereby overcome their pride and fall in Him. Jesus Christ is the object of the individual's faith, and therefore the basis of that faith. The act of faith is the individual's acknowledgment, recognition, and confession. Faith takes in this sense a cognitive character, as God's awakening power in the individual.

(IV/2) In the community, the Holy Spirit is the "quickening" power of God by whom Jesus Christ builds and upholds the community, His body, in the world. As its Lord, the community is grown, sustained, and ordered as the communion of the saints sanctified in Him, acting as a "provisional representation of the sanctification of all humanity and human life as it has taken place in Him." Barth reflects on the true Church, the growth of the community, its upholding (sustaining), and its order.

In the individual, the Holy Spirit is the quickening power of God through whom Jesus Christ gives the individual freedom to love as God has loved, to overcome sloth and misery. Barth develops a Christian understanding of love as *agape,* as opposed to *eros* love. He works from a basis in the self-giving love of God revealed in Jesus Christ, developing the act of love in the individual within the community, and the manner of love as a love which alone counts, triumphs, and endures.

(IV/3) In the community, the Holy Spirit is the "enlightening" power of God by whom Jesus Christ sends the community into the world. God entrusts the Church with the ministry of His own prophetic office, as witnesses to the truth. The community is then the "provisional representation of the calling of all humanity and indeed of all creatures as it has taken place in Him." Jesus Christ sends the Church in the enlightening power of the Holy Spirit out among humanity. The Church is ordained to confess Him before all, to call the world to Him and make known the truth of the gospel. To proclaim that the covenant between God and humanity is fulfilled in Jesus Christ.

In the individual, the Holy Spirit is the enlightening power of God through whom Jesus Christ overcomes the falsehood and condemnation of the individual by calling them to hope, in confidence, patience, and joyful expectation of "His new coming to consummate the revelation of the will of God fulfilled in Him."

FINAL REMARKS

We have hardly scratched the surface of the depth and beauty of this volume with our brief summary. This volume is without a doubt my favorite from the *Church Dogmatics*, not only because in it here the gospel is on full and joyous display. Because Barth presents such an exhaustive and magisterial presentation of the central message of Christianity, *God with us*. It is rightly called a mini-dogmatics. Barth himself called it the heart of all theology, "To fail here is to fail everywhere. To be on the right track here makes it impossible to be completely mistaken in the whole." (*CD* IV/1, ix) You can sense Barth's careful attention to the matter of reconciliation on every page. It is undoubtedly Barth at his best.

SIGNIFICANCE: If the Church took seriously the subtle but radical proposals found in Barth's doctrine of reconciliation, it would drastically alter the way we talk about the core message of our faith. In proclaiming the gospel, we are not threatening the world with damnation, nor are we condemning it with sin. Instead, we declare the gracious and joyful announcement: God has taken up our cause in Jesus Christ, He has put to death our misery and sin, and He has created a new world in the resurrection. The history of Jesus Christ is *our* history, the history of what God has done in grace for the whole world. In Him, we are reconciled, justified, healed, and called to share God's life with Him. In Him, we are children of God, loved and cherished and brought home to the fellowship God enjoys in Godself as Father, Son, and Holy Spirit. This is *good news* in the midst of a world drowning beneath the weigh of so much bad news. This is the *one true* good news, the chief end of our existence, that we might be in fellowship with the God who came to us, who sought and found us in our darkness, who loved us so much to hazard His own being as God for our sakes, to redeem us. There is no dark side to the gospel. It is not a fearful *maybe*, *if*, or *but*. No, there is only God's *Yes* to us, God's affirmation of our being and God's desire never to be God without us. Barth's doctrine of reconciliation, if taken seriously, would change the way we speak about God and the good news; it would change the very nature of our witness as Christians. This is perhaps Barth's most radical proposal, with far-reaching pastoral and evangelical implications. It is simply the call to return to the gospel, to proclaim the good news as truly *good news* once again.

SIDEBAR: LIMITED ATONEMENT AND CALVIN'S HORRIBLE DECREE

For Barth, the doctrines of limited atonement and Calvin's "horrible decree" are nonstarters for virtually the same reason. Barth rejects these notions for their attempt to go behind or above the *revealed* will of God in Jesus Christ, to seek after a higher or deeper *hidden* will in God beyond the person of Jesus Christ. In this sense, we are up once again against Barth's rejection of the hidden God. For Barth, there is no God behind the back of Jesus Christ, and this includes a *will* of God.

So when the doctrine of limited atonement and Calvin's doctrine of double predestination postulates a will of God that limits the love of God for all humanity as revealed in Jesus Christ, turning God's unequivocally revealed *Yes* into a mysterious and hidden *maybe,* it is a fatal error and therefore a grave nonstarter. Furthermore, Barth rejects both doctrines because they read *into* the Scriptures something foreign to it, and are not doctrines based *out of* the Bible itself. We'll briefly explain both errors in this chapter.

As we've seen in the doctrine of reconciliation, sin should never be given predominance over the reconciliation achieved in Jesus Christ. Sin is to be considered only after the fact, as the shadow to the light of the fulfilled covenant. The error of both limited atonement and of double predestination is that of taking the mystery of iniquity far too seriously as the *beginning* point or the basis for doing theology. Barth refuses to take seriously that which Christ has overcome in His life, death, and resurrection. It's not that sin is not a serious thing in itself, but rather that sin in all its seriousness is never anything more than that which has been overcome in Jesus Christ.

Both doctrines seek after a higher will in God to explain the sinfulness of humanity, but Barth refuses to *rationalize* the mystery of iniquity and instead allows it to remain a mystery. Barth does not give sin a foothold over the revealed divine will. This is at the core behind Barth's rejection of both doctrines. Barth supports this by arguing that each doctrine originates by imposing preconceived notions *into* the Bible rather than learning the truth *from* the Bible.

Barth warns about this in *CD* II/2, about how serious a mistake it is to base a doctrine of election upon the "datum of experience, presumed or actual" (*CD* II/2, 38). That is to say, to base a doctrine on our experience with human beings who reject grace, determining in our own judgment that God must also reject them in their rejection of Him. Barth writes further on how this "datum of experience," wrongly implemented as the basis for a doctrine of election, in turn falsely interprets the Scriptures by their *own* judgment and not by God's. Barth warns that "Scripture must not be brought in simply as an interpretation of the facts of the case given by our own judgement" (*CD* II/2, 39). Barth then quotes H. Otten who, in a sharply critical statement, describes the error Calvin fell into with his doctrine of election, "At the very outset, before he consulted the Bible [Calvin had] reached a decision which—quite independently of the answer of Scripture—determined the character of his outlook on predestination in accordance with the question put by experience." And to this Barth notes, "But that is the very thing which should not happen" (*CD* II/2, 41).

When sin is taken too seriously as the unspoken basis for a doctrine of election or limited atonement, this is the inevitable result. If we interpret the Scriptures on the basis of our experience with sin, rather than on the basis of God's Word itself, we interpret God's will according to our experience of sin. In this sense, both double predestination and limited atonement inject into the Bible a presupposed conclusion foreign to what it actually says. In plain terms, Barth rejects both limited atonement and Calvin's horrible decree because these are not taken *from* the Scriptures but are *read into* the Scriptures.

Fundamentally, it is the rejection of a *hidden* will of God that forces Barth to reject both the doctrines of limited atonement and Calvin's horrible decree. Barth perceives a hidden will of God in Calvin's "absolute decree." Barth writes:

> There is no such thing as a *decretum absolutum* [an absolute decree]. There is no such thing as a will of God apart from the will of Jesus Christ.
>
> — CD II/2, 115

> The electing God of Calvin is a *Deus nudus absconditus* [hidden God] [...] All the dubious features of Calvin's doctrine result from the basic failing that in the last analysis he separates God and Jesus Christ.
>
> — CD II/2, 111

Bringing all this together—the rejection of the hidden God, Barth's doctrine of election and reconciliation, and the scriptural failing of these doctrines—it should now be clear why Barth rejects these two fundamental aspects of classical Calvinism. Calvin ultimately separates God and Jesus Christ. Yet Barth insists on speaking of God exclusively in terms of Jesus Christ. This is their fundamental difference.

In closing, Bruce McCormack summarizes this fundamental difference between Calvin's and Barth's respective doctrines of election. McCormack writes:

> Calvin's mistake was not simply that he understood predestination to entail a pre-temporal division of the human race into two camps. That is only his most conspicuous error. But the root of

the difference between Calvin and Barth lies at a much deeper level—at the level of divine ontology [being]. The electing God, Barth argues, is not an unknown 'X'. He is a God whose very being—already in eternity—is determined, defined, by what he reveals himself to be in Jesus Christ, viz. [in other words] a God of love and mercy towards the whole human race. That is what Barth means for us to understand when he says that Jesus Christ is the Subject of election.

— Bruce McCormack: "Grace and Being" The Cambridge Companion to Karl Barth, 97-8.

God is not an unknown "X" but the God who makes Godself known in Jesus Christ. Calvin's limitation of God's will to include only some in the plan for salvation posits a mysterious God who differs from the God revealed in the life and work of Jesus Christ for all humanity. It *excludes* where God in Christ *includes*.

SERMON: THE DIVINE LIFE

In a sermon, Barth proclaims a profound reality of the gospel central to the doctrine of the atonement. God did not will to be God without us, but to exist in divinity *with* humanity, to be our God. This "God with us" of the gospel is for Barth one of the major ideas in the message of reconciliation. Barth writes:

> *I live.* When spoken by Jesus this means: 'I live my divine life *for you.* I live it fully by loving you. Without you I do not care to be the Son of God or to enjoy my divine life. I live it fully by pouring it out. Without reticence or reservation I give it away for you. I live my divine life by taking your place, the place that is allowed to you. I become what you are (not just some of you, but all of you), a prisoner, a convict, sentenced to death. This I do, by the power of my divine life spent for you, that the darkness and perplexity, the sorrow, anxiety and despair, the sin and guilt of your petty, wicked and miserable life may be cancelled out, and your own death may once and for all be extinguished and annihilated. In this giving of myself, in the saving power I live my life, my divine life.'

— DELIVERANCE TO THE CAPTIVES, 30

After considering our being cancelled and put to death as sinners in Jesus Christ, Barth highlights the resurrection as the "you will live also" of the good news. He writes:

> It is all-important now that not one among us consider himself excluded, either too great or too insignificant or too godless. It is all important that each one of us consider himself included, a partaker of God's mercy in the life of our Lord as revealed in his resurrection from the dead on Easter morning. It is all important that we believe humbly yet courageously that we are those born again in him to a living hope: *You will live also.*
>
> — IBID., 33

This is an insight Barth often emphasizes when he works out the doctrine of reconciliation. The doctrine of reconciliation is primarily a statement *about God*—about the God who does not will to be God without us, who became God with us, whose life takes up our life and includes it, whose history in Jesus is our history. Barth writes in *CD* IV/1:

> The divine being and life and act takes place with ours, and it is only as the divine takes place that ours takes place. To put it in the simplest way, what unites God and us men is that He does not will to be God without us, that He creates us rather to share with us and therefore with our being and life and act His own incomparable being and life and act, that He does not allow His history to be His and ours ours, but causes them to take place as a common history. ...Salvation, fulfillment, perfect being means— and this is what created being does not have in itself—being which has a part in the being of God, from which and to which it is; not a divinised being but a being which is hidden in God, and in that sense (distinct from God and secondary) eternal being.
>
> — CD IV/1, 7-8

That God gives Godself to humanity in Jesus Christ is the good news of *Immanuel,* and it is a central idea in Barth's doctrine of reconciliation.

In giving Godself, God does not give merely a part of Godself or a small aspect of divinity, but God gives *Godself*—the extravagant gift which surpasses all else.

> God for us men. God who in His triune being, in the fulness of His Godhead, is Himself the essence of all favour, the source and stream and sea of everything that is good, of all light and life and joy. To say God is to say eternal benefit. [...] He makes Himself the companion of man. He does not merely give him something, however great. He gives Himself, and in so doing gives him all things.

— CD IV/1, 40

SERMON: HAVE YOU HEARD THE NEWS?

In another sermon, Barth offers an analogy on how to proclaim the gospel as a *fact,* and not merely as an abstract opportunity (or worse, as a threat!). We do not proclaim the *possibility* of saving yourself if you do A, B, and C, but the accomplished reconciliation of humanity in Jesus Christ, the fulfillment of the covenant in Him. Therefore, we call men and women to *wake up* to this reality, to see and believe the good news. The good news is not a good *opportunity*; it is truly good *news.*

Did you read in the paper recently that two Japanese soldiers were found in the Philippines, who had not yet heard, or did not believe, that the war had ended fourteen years ago? They continue to hide in some jungle and shoot at everybody who dares approach them. Strange people, aren't they? Well, we are such people when we refuse to perceive and to hold true what the Easter message declares to be the meaning of the Easter story. Sin and death are conquered; God's free gift prevails, his gift of eternal life for us all. Shall we not very humbly pay heed to this message? Death–but life! 'Wake up, sleeper, and rise from the dead, that Jesus Christ may be your light!' He, Jesus Christ, who made our history his own and, in a marvelous turn-about, made his wondrous history our own! He in whom the kingdom of the devil is already destroyed! In whom the kingdom of God and of his peace has already come, to us, to you and me, to us all, on the earth and in the whole world! Amen.

— Deliverance to the Captives, 149-150

8

THE CHURCH AND ETHICS

SUMMARY: Barth's theology has a particular focus on both the Church and on theological ethics. Barth refused to speak theologically *in abstracto* (in the abstract) without at once speaking ethically or ecclesiastically. This twofold emphasis is noteworthy as a consistent driving force behind his theology. Barth's theological ethic is an ethic of grace in which we are called in freedom to be who we are in Jesus Christ.

IN BARTH'S OWN WORDS:

In substituting the word Church for Christian in the title [of the *Church Dogmatics*], I have tried to set a good example of restraint in the lightheaded use of the great word 'Christian' against which I have protested. But materially I have also tried to show that from the very outset dogmatics is not a free science. It is bound to the sphere of the Church, where alone it is possible and meaningful.

— CD I/1, XII-XIII

Implicitly, dogmatics must always be ethical as well. If we had not come to realise and see this in all those elements of a Christian knowledge of creation, we should have been indulging in empty speculation and therefore engaged in futile labour.

— CD III/4, 32

The questions of ethics and Christian mission are not peripheral for [Barth]. They are not even to be treated as separate loci or doctrines at the end of theology. By his ingenious organization of his doctrinal structure, Barth has made it possible to incorporate ethics and ecclesiology as continuing themes throughout the whole structure. He maintains that the final import of every aspect of Christian faith and doctrine has not been clarified until its ethical impact has been brought to light. Also, the Church for Barth has no distinctive reality except as it is rooted at every point in the living Christ himself.

— Arnold B. Come: An Introduction to Barth's
Dogmatics for Preachers, 18

For Barth, freedom in its most proper sense is the confirmation in our decision of God's decision for us. It is the freedom of the human covenant partner of God. By contrast, natural freedom is the neutral capacity to choose one action or another. Barth explicitly denies that this capacity to choose is freedom in the proper sense. [...] We decide for God's decision for us. Our nature is suited to be our being as God's covenant partner. [...] Ethics for Barth involves confirming ontically, in our existence as acting subjects, to what we already are ontologically, affirming in our life conduct (ontic) who and what we are as creatures who share the humanity of Jesus Christ (ontological). Far from imposing a requirement that is alien to our humanity, the command of God requires the concrete realization of our humanity.

— Gerald McKenny: The Analogy of Grace, 12-3, 16

Twofold emphasis

The final major idea we will discuss is a twofold emphasis in Barth's thought. We have already discussed both points of emphasis since Barth stresses them over and over again from the first volume of the *Dogmatics* to the very last. This is Barth's dual emphasis on the Church and theological ethics. Rather than presenting an abstract doctrine of God, humanity, and salvation, Barth presents his *Dogmatics* within the context of the community called by God to be the earthly-historical form of His existence (His body), and with consideration towards the command of God included in that call, the task of theological ethics.

It is not by mistake that Barth calls his dogmatics *Church Dogmatics*. The primary purpose of these large volumes, for Barth, was to serve the Church in its proclamation of the gospel. It is also not by mistake that Barth concludes each volume of the *Church Dogmatics* with a treatment of ethics. Ethics are an integral aspect of theology for Barth, inseparable to the whole task of dogmatics. He did not imagine his theology to be like a cloud up in the sky. Theology is a human work, a timely work, a task which includes special care over how we are to live, answering the ever important question, primarily a theological question, "What shall we do?"

I want to highlight these two points of emphasis as we close out our discussion of Barth's major ideas. It would be a severe mistake and ultimately a failure to understand Barth correctly if we were to neglect these aspects of his thought. It has become common today to understand Barth in terms of his doctrines alone—as if he ever hoped to treat these doctrines in isolation from the Church and the command of God. Barth's commitment to the Church and to ethics as a special theological task is a much-needed dedication, especially today in such an increasingly individualistic, isolated society.

Karl Barth and the Church

In commending Barth to preachers, Arnold B. Come writes, "Barth's whole unique theological formulation had its origin and rise from the specific problem of the sermon" (*An Introduction to Barth's* Dogmatics *for Preachers,* 14). Barth himself confessed, "My whole theology, you see, is fundamentally a theology for pastors. It grew out of my own situation when I had to teach and preach and counsel a little" (*Final Testimonies,* 23). Barth's theology is a theology *for the Church.*

Following Barth's theological schooling under Harnack and Herrmann, two of the leading proponents of liberal theology at the time, he was assigned a pastoral position in the small town of Safenwil. For ten years Barth regularly engaged in the task of preaching and teaching in that small town, during which he likely wrote more than five-hundred sermons. It was during this period that the dire need to return to the "strange new world within the Bible" emerged. Barth became concerned with the task of preaching, that daunting task of saying *something about God,* and began to understand the immense difficulty this entailed.

This search led to Barth's famous first edition of *The Epistle to the Romans* in 1919. Together with his life-long friend Eduard Thurneysen, Barth relearned his theological ABCs by reading and interpreting the Scriptures more thoughtfully than he had before.

Barth's entire theological enterprise was constructed in relation to the Church. During his lifetime, even while acting as a professor, he was heavily involved in the life of the Church. He saw his *Dogmatics* primarily as a service to the Church of Jesus Christ. It was not by mistake that he changed the title of his earlier, "false start" dogmatics (*Christian Dogmatics*) to the more appropriate *Church Dogmatics.* There is no such thing as an isolated *Christian* dogmatics which is not at once a *Church* dogmatics. Theology isn't written up in the air apart from the life of the Church, but only as a service to the Church; at its core, dogmatic theology is a critical reflection on the message proclaimed by the Church: the gospel of Jesus Christ.

This is why Barth's theology cannot be understood as a free, speculative science, like that of a philosophy which has no set ties or allegiances. Instead, Barth's theology is best understood within the context he wished it to be understood in: the Church. His is a theology which finds its home here in the community of Jesus Christ and nowhere else.

KARL BARTH AND THEOLOGICAL ETHICS

The second emphasis we have to note that characterizes Barth's theology is his attention to the problem of ethics as a *central* problem for dogmatic theology and not merely a side-issue. Barth first cemented his rejection of liberal theology because of his dismay over the "ethical failure" of his former professors. It was a *political* and *ethical* problem which Barth identified in liberalism that lead to his rejection of it, not solely a theological one. Barth describes this best himself:

> On that very day 'ninety-three German intellectuals issued a terrible manifesto, identifying themselves before all the world with the war policy of Kaiser Wilhelm II and Chancellor Bethmann-Hollweg. For me it was almost worse than the violation of Belgian neutrality. And to my dismay, among the signatories I discovered the names of almost all my German teachers (with the honorable exception of Martin Rade). It was like the twilight of the gods when I saw the reaction of Harnack, Hermann, Rade, Eucken and company to the new situation', and discovered how religion and scholarship could be changed completely, 'into intellectual 42 cm cannons'. [...] Their 'ethical failure' indicated that 'their exegetical and dogmatic presuppositions could not be in order'.

— BUSCH: KARL BARTH, 81

Not only did Barth's theological enterprise develop in the context of preaching, demanding a new attention to the Scriptures which resulted in his *Romans* commentary, but Barth's theological enterprise began with profound ethical and political concerns. He recognized from the start that theology and ethics are not isolated from each other, but rightly saw how the theological failures of his teachers lead to their ethical failures. There is no practical problem which is not at once a theological problem, and no theological problem which is not at once a practical problem.

Barth wrote his *Dogmatics* with special attention to the ethical problems of theology. There is not a volume of the *Church Dogmatics* which does not contain some treatment of ethics.

In *CD* I/2, within paragraph §22 there is the sub-heading entitled "Dogmatics as Ethics" which addresses the wrongful displacement of ethics from the work of theological consideration; and there is also a treatment in §18 of the command to love God and your neighbor. In *CD* II/2, under the chapter heading "The Command of God" (which makes up a third of the entire volume), Barth addresses the command of God within the context of the doctrine of election. In *CD* III/4, Barth goes even further in his ethical focus by dedicating an entire volume (of nearly 700 pages) to treat the special ethical considerations of the doctrine of creation. And finally, in *CD* IV, Barth planned an entire volume (which he never finished) if not multiple volumes on the ethics of the Christian life. Barth was only able to begin work on *CD* IV/4, on the Christian life founded on Baptism, but planned a special ethical volume on the Lord's Prayer as the fulfillment of the Christian life, and the Lord's Supper as the renewal of the Christian life in thanksgiving (see *The Christian Life* for lecture fragments of these sections). There can be no doubt that in each volume Barth gave special and careful attention to ethics as an integral aspect of dogmatic theology.

From start to finish, Barth's theology was never meant to be read as an abstract speculation, but deeply ingrained in his theological work special attention was given to the ethical question, "What shall we do?" Perhaps more so than any other theologian before or since, Karl Barth was an *ethical* theologian just as he was a theologian for the *Church*. We would do him a disservice not to make a note of this dual emphasis while discussing his theology.

Since we have already briefly given an outline of Barth's work on ecclesiology in *CD* IV, as it was integrated with the doctrine of the Holy Spirit and reconciliation, we will primarily examine in this chapter Barth's unique theological ethics as an ethic of grace which calls us to be who we already are in Jesus Christ.

AN ETHIC OF GRACE AND FREEDOM; BE WHO YOU ARE IN JESUS CHRIST

Barth's theological ethics is as radical as some of his most ground-breaking theological insights, though it is often appreciated far less. What are the major characteristics of Barth's ethics? While we won't tackle a complete treatment of Barth's ethics, we will briefly sketch a few of its most significant characteristics.

Barth's theological ethics is not about doing good things and avoiding bad things; instead, as an ethic centered on divine grace, Barth argues that God alone reveals and accomplishes that which is truly good in the person of Jesus Christ on our behalf. This is not an ethical command to work hard and strive towards a moral goal, but it is an ethic centered on God's grace which defines what is good and accomplishes that good in our place. As such, Barth's ethic is primarily focused on the person of Jesus Christ. It is not an ethic with human beings at its center. Theological ethics do not center on what *we* must do to accomplish the good, but on what God has done on our behalf. We participate in obedience and gratitude in God's ethics by grace through faith in Jesus Christ who accomplishes and determines God's ethical good in our humanity. It is important to note that this is not an ethic which God completes over our heads, but an ethic which becomes actual in our humanity through our participation by grace in Christ's accomplished good. We echo and repeat in our lives the good which God has determined as good and has accomplished already for us in Jesus Christ.

There is a parallel here between this and Barth's rejection of natural theology. Just as Barth rejects the possibility of a natural theology, so in a similar way Barth rejects the possibility of a *natural* ethic known or accomplished apart from the grace of God in Jesus Christ. We have seen how the doctrine of grace drastically changes the way Barth thinks about the knowledge of God, and in the same way, Barth forms a theological ethic which is on par with the doctrine of God's grace. Barth's theological ethics is a *Christological* ethic, and as such, it is an ethic of grace.

There is a distinction between *human* ethics and *God's* ethics. Barth is critical of any ethic that places human beings and our (false) "ability" to determine what is good and evil at the center of its reflection. He goes so far as to call such a human-centric ethic a *sinful* construction, saying it "coincides exactly with the conception of sin" (*CD* II/2, 518). He likens it to the serpent's temptation of Adam and Eve in the garden. Barth sharply remarks:

> An ethics that thinks it can know and set forth the command of God, the Creator, plants itself upon the throne of God: it stops and poisons the wells and is more fraught with peril to the Christian life than all cinemas and dancing-saloons piled together.
>
> — THE HOLY SPIRIT AND THE CHRISTIAN LIFE, 10

It is clear, for Barth, that theological ethics is not centered around the question of what human beings determine to be ethical. Only God is the judge of good and evil. True theological ethics are *God's* ethics, centered around what God determines and accomplishes as "the good" in our place.

———

What this ethic looks like in the practical sense is the command to, "Be who you are in Jesus Christ." McKenny notes, 'The command of God does nothing more (and nothing less) than summon us to be in our life conduct what we already are thanks to what Christ has done in our place" (*The Analogy of Grace,* 166). This is perhaps best explained in relation to Barth's concept of human freedom. Freedom, for Barth, is not unbound, limitless freedom such as the possibility of deciding between good or evil. Such a decision would ultimately become another kind of bondage. The original sin of Adam and Eve was to seek after their own independent ethic against God's ethics as the Lord who alone decides what is good and evil. We are not free to do "whatever we want" in an ethically speculative sense. Freedom means freedom to be who we are created and elected to be in Jesus Christ; that is, to be covenant partners with God, to be in a relationship with God, and to participate in His triune life. We are created to be this and only this, and when we are who we are (who we are *in Him*) we are free from what we are not.

Freedom does not mean infinite possibilities; it is the act of being who we already are in Jesus Christ. There is no "ultimate freedom" for Barth because this in itself is a kind of bondage. God's grace does not destroy nature but directs and empowers our nature to be what God originally created us to be. Grace empowers our humanity to be a *true* humanity, to be human beings in fellowship with God. Freedom is the free decision for God's decision for us, it is saying Yes to God's original Yes to us. Freedom excludes the possibility of saying No—as strange as that sounds—because saying No means ultimately becoming unfree by choosing to be what we cannot be, what we no longer are in truth; namely, the sinner that God put to death in Jesus Christ. True freedom means only saying Yes to be who we are in Him, to be God's covenant partner, to be the object of God's love in fellowship with Him. This is the command of God: *be who you are.*

The command of God is not that we *must do* good in order to *be* good, but that we *may do* good *because* we already *are* good (sanctified) in Him. We are commanded in obedience and gratitude to do the good which God has already revealed and accomplished on our behalf in Jesus Christ, to echo and repeat Christ's accomplished good, because this is who we are in Him.

EXAMPLES FROM BARTH

We'll now briefly look at a few passages where Barth highlights this ethical command as the gracious call to be who you are in Jesus Christ.

First, in contrasting our sinful human-centric ethic with God's ethic, Barth writes:

> The grace of God protests against all man-made ethics as such. But it protests positively. It does not only say No to man. It also says Yes. But it does so by completing its own answer to the ethical problem in active refutation, conquest and destruction of all human answers to it. It does this by revealing in Jesus Christ the human image with which Adam was created to correspond and could no longer do so when he sinned, when he became ethical man. …The sanctification of man, the fact that he is claimed by God, the fulfillment of his predetermination in his self-determination to obedience, the judgement of God on man and His command to him in its actual concrete fulfillment—they all take place here in Jesus Christ. The good is done here—really the good as understood critically—beyond all that merely pretends to be called good. …This is how the good is done here. This is how the ethical question is answered here—in Jesus Christ. What has taken place in this way—in antithesis and contrast to all human ethics—is divine ethics.
>
> — CD II/2, 517

There is an ethic which humans attempt in themselves, but Barth's point here is that grace destroys our ethic and replaces it with God's ethic, revealed and accomplished in Jesus Christ. Barth continues:

> We cannot act as if we had to ask and decide of ourselves what the good

is and how we can achieve it; as if we were free to make this or that answer as the one that appears to us to be right. …When we speak of ethics, the term cannot include anything more than this confirmation of the truth of the grace of God as it is addressed to man. If dogmatics, if the doctrine of God, is ethics, this means necessarily and decisively that it is the attestation of that *divine* ethics, the attestation of the good of the command issued to Jesus Christ and fulfilled by Him. There can be no question of any other good in addition to this. Other apparent goods are good only in dependence on this good.

— CD II/2, 518

Barth is again destroying the false foundations for a human ethic constructed apart from the gracious acts of God in Jesus Christ, and displacing it with the divine ethic made known as it is accomplished in Him.

Second, Barth emphasizes the completion of this ethic, Jesus Christ acting rightly in our place before God, upholding the covenant faithfulness to the Father in Himself, and accordingly doing "the good" on our behalf which only God knows and can do. Barth writes:

The Word and work of God as such is also the sanctification of man, the establishment and revelation of the divine law. What right conduct is for man is determined absolutely in the right conduct of God. It is determined in Jesus Christ. He is the electing God and elected man in One. But He is also the sanctifying God and sanctified man in One. In His person God has acted rightly towards us. And in the same person man has also acted rightly for us. In His person God has judged man and restored him to His image. And in His person again man has reconstituted himself in the divine likeness. We do not need any other image but this: neither another image of God nor another image of man and his right conduct; neither another Gospel nor another Law. In the one image of Jesus Christ we have both the Gospel which reconciles us with God and illumines us and consoles us, and the Law which in contradistinction to all the laws which we ourselves find or fabricate really bind and obligates us. This is the Law to which theological ethics clings. It is ethics of grace or it is not theological ethics.

— CD II/2, 538-9

Third, in terms of human freedom, Barth claims, "The command of God sets man free" (*CD* II/2, 586). This shows why Barth contrasted God's own ethic and our human ethics. A human ethics is centered around "do this and not that," but God's ethic is about the positive freedom we are granted to be who we are, to live in fellowship with God. Barth's ethical treatment moves us away from God's command as a forceful "you must" to God's command as a gracious "you may." Barth elaborates:

The command of God wills only that we, for our part, accept that God in Jesus Christ is so kind that He accepts us just as we are. It wills only that we make use of the given permission by the grace of God to be what we are, and therefore that we do not leave again the shelter which the faithfulness of God has given us against the infernal tempest of all other outward and inward claims, that we do not do again what Adam did, that we do not play the lord and therefore become masterless and therefore helpless and defenseless. The command of God orders us to be free. How can it be otherwise? The command is only the form of the Gospel of God, in virtue of which—not in and by ourselves, but in and by Jesus Christ—we are free.

— CD II/2, 588

When Barth says that God empowers us to be who we are, he does not mean who we are in our sin, but who we are *in reality*, which means exclusively who we are in Jesus Christ. For Barth, this is the only *true* reality, against our false reality marred by sin. This is a key aspect of Barth's theological ethics. We are not sinners in Jesus Christ. Our true nature is hidden in Him as new creatures, justified, sanctified, and adopted into fellowship with God. To be who we are is to be who we are in Him. It is therefore not a freedom to do whatever we want but to be who we truly are, who we could never become on our own, to be a child of God adopted in Jesus Christ to fellowship with God. This is *true* freedom, against our false perception of freedom as an infinite possibility.

SIGNIFICANCE: In a modern world where the individual is yet again elevated to a new point of pride and isolation and falsehood, pretending to master the world and to be its lord, Barth's reminder that we must be people in a community who follow God's gracious ethic is nothing short of revolutionary. While it appears on the surface to be a simple emphasis, Barth has laid the foundation for a community that does not separate knowledge from ethics, theology from fellowship—a holistic community committed to Jesus Christ in word and deed. The gospel heals humanity step by step, humanizing human beings: against individualism, it brings a community, against self-centered living it brings fellowship, against self-righteous judgments it provides an ethic, against hostile wills it brings discipleship and peace. Barth's integration of the community and the task of ethics reminds us to be doers of the word, together.

SERMON: YOU MAY

The Reformation rightly emphasized the doctrine of grace, but it failed to implement that doctrine in the problem of ethics consistently. Barth's theological ethic corrects this inconsistency. Luther's "Law and Gospel" is reversed by Barth to be the "Gospel and Law," giving grace preeminence. His theological ethics is a return to grace as the beginning of all God's ways and works, which includes the determination of "the good" and its accomplishment in our humanity.

In a sermon on Jeremiah 31:33 ("I will put my law within them, and I will write it upon their hearts."), Barth speaks about the gracious command of God as a "you may" instead of a "you must." Barth begins by contrasting all other laws with God's law:

> My dear brothers and sisters, I do not think that I am wrong if I assume that the word *law* has something oppressive and unpleasant about it for most, indeed probably for all of you. [...] There is only *one* law where things are different: a law which does not cause distress but gives joy, which does not lead us into a strange sinister country, but into our homeland—only *one* law which does not restrict us and so violate our freedom and become troublesome and annoying to us, but rather sets us free [...] The

one completely different law is the law of *God,* that is to say if he
puts it within us, writes it upon our *hearts.*

— CALL FOR GOD, 20-1

Barth then asks hypothetically what it would be like if God had *not*
written the law on our hearts:

Just what is it that God's law says to us if he does *not* put it within
us, does *not* write it in our hearts? In that case, it says to us sharply
and violently and terrifyingly: You *shall!* […] You shall, you shall,
you shall! This is how God's law sounds, that is what we hear if
God does not put his law within us, and does not write it upon
our hearts. That is how we hear his voice from the midst of that
cloud. […] Such, then, is our situation without God's free grace;
if the law of God speaks from the cloud, if he does not put his law
within us and does not write it upon our hearts.

— IBID., 21-3

This is the kind of ethic we construct in our own strength when we
ignore divine revelation and seek after God's commandment anywhere
else but in Jesus who alone reveals and does in our humanity that which is
truly good.

Barth continues, "But that is precisely his promise. [To write His law
on our hearts.] He wishes to do this, and he will do it" (ibid., 23). And
when we find that God's law has been written on our hearts, when we
learn what *God's* ethic is where God has revealed it to us in Jesus, then we
hear a different word. "No longer does it say 'You shall!', but *'You may'."*
Barth describes what obedience to this law looks like:

'Fulfillment of a must', as they say in the eastern states, is by no
means the obedience which God requires. Obedience means: to
be *permitted* to obey, in *freedom,* to obey of one's own accord, to
choose the good and avoid the evil of one's own accord.

— IBID., 23

Here is the driving difference between Barth's ethic of grace and all human ethics of works; the former relies on *God's* ethic (written upon our hearts), and the latter relies on a human ethic. God's law is not the command, "You must." God's command is a gracious, "You may!" It is a call to *freedom*.

What is this freedom *for*? Barth beautifully summarizes what it is that God's law demands of us:

> What his *command* says when we hear and understand it properly is this: Allow yourself now quite simply to be loved by me, and love me in return. That, just that, is 'the good', if you do it. That, just that, is the root, the meaning, the force of all Ten Commandments. 'Love and do what you like' said a great father of the Church [Augustine]. A bold saying, but a true one. For that's what it's like. Whoever allows himself to be loved by God, and on the strength of that may love him in return, and because of this love does what he requires, is certainly doing what is right. That is what is written.
>
> What God's *prohibition* says is this: Just do not resist any longer the love in which I love you and you may love me. … If you resist it and do not allow yourself to be loved, if you make no use of the freedom by which you too may love, then you may be the finest, the most excellent, the most serious of fellows: yet the best you do and plan will be false and perverted. That is what is written.
>
> — IBID., 24

What is the meaning of our existence? Who are we fundamentally as human beings? We exist to be loved by God, to love God in return on the strength of Christ's love. We exist to live in fellowship with God and with each other. This is our true self. I summarized in the previous chapter Barth's ethic of grace as the call to "Be who you are," and these quotations reinforce that point. To be who you are in Jesus Christ is to be the beloved child of God you were created to be, to live in joyful fellowship with God.

Barth further notes of this ethic of grace, "As I said at the beginning:

this is God's work and gift to us, his free grace. But that means that this *is* his free grace; he *creates* it, he *bestows* it" (ibid., 25). And finally, in summary: "You may: that is the new and true commandment, the law of God put within us and written in our hearts. Simply and straightforwardly it is our freedom to enjoy him, and obediently to do his will" (ibid.).

SIDEBAR: POLITICAL PREFERENCE FOR THE POOR

NOTE: This sidebar was initially published for an online blog-conference in 2018, and has been slightly revised for inclusion in this book. I regretted overlooking Barth's political thought in the first edition of this book. Thus, in its second edition, I have included this essay to highlight some of Barth's political convictions. See George Hunsinger's Karl Barth and Radical Politics *for a broader view of Barth's politics.*

We cannot rightly claim to follow the way of Jesus Christ without following him into solidarity with the poor and oppressed. God's self-humiliation in Christ necessarily entails political preference for the poor. What might this look like in a world of rapidly increasing economic inequality? The Church today cannot remain indifferent. We must follow the way of Jesus Christ into self-humiliation and take sides, entering into solidarity with the poor and weak by standing against the systemic oppression of the impoverished.

Liberation theology popularized "God's preferential option for the poor." While there are a number of differences between Karl Barth and liberation theology, they both considered preferential care for the poor to be a Christian obligation. Although Barth is sometimes seen in an apolitical light, his theology was profoundly political from beginning to end. As he admitted towards the end of his life, "[M]y theology always had a strong political side, explicit or implicit" (*Final Testimonies,* 24).

It is well known that Barth was politically active in his early days as a pastor in Safenwil and with the Confessing Church, but it is often mistakenly implied that Barth's theology was later de-politicized when he left Germany for Basel. The truth is, Barth's entire theological project is politically oriented, even if it became more *implicitly* political later in his career. The example I want to examine to show this is the connection between Barth's Christology (particularly in *CD* IV/1) and his political preference for the poor.

Barth's doctrine of reconciliation stresses God's self-humiliation in Christ, and from this, it is only a small step to see the connection between God's self-humiliation and the preferential option for the poor. It is precisely because God became a man in Jesus Christ, thereby taking up our darkness and sin as His own, that God stands in solidarity with the poor for the sake of the liberation of all humanity. That is to say, for Barth, God's self-humiliation reveals God's inherent preference for the poor—not simply *against* the rich but also *for* their liberation. But this movement towards liberation must begin with the Church's preference for the poor in the political sphere. Barth writes:

> The Church is witness of the fact that the Son of man came to seek and to save the lost. And this implies that—casting all false impartiality aside—the Church must concentrate first on the lower and lowest levels of human society. The poor, the socially and economically weak and threatened, will always be the object of its primary and particular concern, and it will always insist on the State's special responsibility for these weaker members of society. That it will bestow its love on them—within the framework of its own task (as part of its service), is one thing and the most important thing; but it must not concentrate on this and neglect the other thing to which it is committed by its political responsibility: the effort to achieve such a fashioning of the law as will make it impossible for 'equality before the law' to become a cloak under which strong and weak, independent and dependent, rich and poor, employers and employees, in fact receive difference

treatment at its hands: the weak being unduly restricted, the strong unduly protected. The Church must stand for social justice in the political sphere. And in choosing between the various socialistic possibilities [...] it will always choose the movement from which it can expect the greatest measure of social justice (leaving all other considerations on one side).

— AGAINST THE STREAM, 36

Jesus Christ is the basis for the Church's preference for the poor, and therefore to neglect the poor is to forsake Christ. It is for Christ's sake that the Church must stand on the side of the poor and oppressed. Barth's well-known Christocentric thought is here applied to the realm of political action. In *Church Dogmatics* volume IV/1, he provides the theological basis for this move when he discusses the self-humiliation of God in Christ. "God chooses condescension." Barth writes, "He chooses humiliation, lowliness and obedience. In this way He illuminates the darkness, opening up that which is closed. In this way He brings help where there is no other help" (*CD* IV/1, 199). With this in mind, notice *why* Barth argues here that the Church must take sides with the oppressed:

Christ was born into poverty in the stable at Bethlehem, and He died in extreme poverty, nailed naked to the Cross. He is, then, the companion, not of the rich men of this world, but of the poor of this world. For that reason He called the poor blessed, and not the rich. For that reason He is here and now always to be found in the company of the hungry, the homeless, the naked, the sick, the prisoners.

— IBID., 246

It is not empty humanism to stress God's preferential option for the poor. For Barth, the Church must take sides with the poor because it is precisely here, in the company of the marginalized, that we find ourselves in the company of Jesus Christ. It is *because* of Barth's devotion to Jesus Christ that Barth calls the Church to stand on the side of the poor and oppressed. It is a conviction based, first and foremost, in Christology. We cannot separate Barth's theology from his political convictions, as George Hunsinger writes, "Those who think they can have Barth's doctrine without his radical politics show that they have yet to understand him" (*Karl Barth and Radical Politics*, xii).

American evangelicalism is beginning to embrace Barth's theology more readily today than it did in his own time, but it has not yet adopted his radical politics. Americans seem to desire his theological revolution without his political revolution, but Barth's theology, rightly understood, is implicitly connected to his political conviction that the Church must stand on the side of the poor and oppressed. We cannot have the one without the other.

Christians should not enter into the public and political spheres for their own sake, but for Christ's sake. In a concrete sense, this means engaging in politics for the sake of the poor and oppressed. Christians who vote, petition, and participate in political discourse selfishly, with only their own interests in mind, have failed to be truly *Christ*ian in their politics, no matter what lip-service they offer to Christian values.

The present economic status quo in America helps only those who are already rich, privileged, and healthy; it actively oppresses those who are impoverished, unwell, or disabled. By either silently or vocally supporting the status quo, the evangelical Church has placed itself on the side of the oppressors rather than the oppressed. It has, in Barth's words, used the cloak of "equality" to support restricting the rights of the poor and maximizing the rights of the successful and wealthy, thus systemically supporting the oppression of the impoverished.

The Church must take a stand against oppression, wherever it may be found, and therefore we must be a consistently critical voice against the status quo. When the status quo remains unchallenged, those who stay silent are complicit in ongoing oppression. The Church must stand in favor of the weak and the small, because Jesus Christ came to seek and save the lost, to befriend sinners, and to take up our poverty as his own.

The Church must take sides and stand in solidarity with the poor and oppressed—*for Christ's sake*. The implicit connection between Barth's Christology and his political convictions lends further support for this call to action. Barth's theology is sharply incongruent with any political system that blatantly mistreats the poor and oppressed members of society.

CONCLUSION: GOD WITH US AND FOR US

I want to end our study with an extended quote from one of Barth's final books, *Evangelical Theology: An Introduction.* This is undoubtedly one of my favorite passages from Barth's work, and thus a fitting summary as we end this book.

> The God of the Gospel is no lonely God, self-sufficient and self-contained. He is no 'absolute' God (in the original sense of absolute, i.e., being detached from everything that is not himself). To be sure, he has no equal beside himself, since an equal would no doubt limit, influence, and determine him. On the other hand, he is not imprisoned by his own majesty, as though he were bound to be no more than the personal (or impersonal) 'wholly other.' By definition, the God of Schleiermacher cannot show mercy. The God of the Gospel can and does. Just as his oneness consists in the unity of his life as Father, Son, and Holy Spirit, so in relation to the reality distinct from him he is free *de jure* and *de facto* to be the God of *man.* He exists neither *next* to man nor merely *above* him, but rather *with* him, *by* him and, most important of all, *for* him. He is *man's* God not only as Lord but also as father, brother, friend; and this relationship implies neither a diminution nor in any way a denial, but, instead, a confirmation and display of his divine essence itself. ...A God who confronted man simply as exalted, distant, and strange, that is,

a divinity without humanity, could only be the God of a *dysangelion,* of a
'bad news' instead of the 'good news.' […]

Many other theologies may be concerned with such exalted,
superhuman, and inhuman gods, who can only be the gods of every sort
of bad news, or *dysangelion.* But the God who is the object of evangelical
theology is just as lowly as he is exalted. He is exalted precisely in his
lowliness. And so his inevitable No is enclosed in his primary Yes to
man. In this way, what God wills for man is a helpful, healing, and
uplifting work, and what he does with him brings peace and joy. Because
of this he is really the God of the *euangelion,* the Evangel, the Word that
is good for man because it is gracious. With its efforts, evangelical
theology responds to this gracious Yes, to God's self-proclamation made
in his friendliness towards man. It is concerned with God as the God of
man, but just for this reason, also with man, as *God's* man. In evangelical
theology, man is absolutely not, as Nietzsche has put it, 'something that
must be overcome.' […] Since it is 'evangelical,' [theology] can by no
means be devoted to an inhuman God, for in that case it would become
legalistic theology. Evangelical theology is concerned with Immanuel,
God with us! Having this God for its object, it can be nothing else but
the most thankful and *happy* science!

— Evangelical Theology, 10-2

It was this quotation that ignited my passion for studying Karl Barth's
theology, and it is still one of my favorites. Barth is a true *evangelical*
theologian, in the original sense of the word. Every time I read Barth, I
am confronted again with what makes the good news so good, I am
reminded of the *joy* of the gospel. The God of the gospel is really the only
subject of Barth's theology: God with us and God for us, Jesus Christ.
This is the God who has said *yes* to us and not no, the God who has determined Godself to be *our* God and not another. Barth's dedication to the
good news of Jesus Christ is what attracts me the most to his theology.
Perhaps more than any other theologian I have read, Barth's work is a
joyful celebration of the gospel of Jesus Christ.

It was this Word which Barth wish to be his final word. Barth said as
much in one of his last public statements, bookended on a radio show
between some of Mozart's finest symphonies:

I am not ultimately at home in theology, in the political world, or even in the Church. These are all preparatory matters. [...] And this brings me to where I am really at home, or, should I say, to him with whom I am at home. Grace itself is only a provisional word. The last word that I have to say as a theologian or a politician is not a concept like grace but a name: Jesus Christ. He is grace and he is the ultimate one beyond world and Church and even theology. We cannot lay hold of him. But we have to do with him. And my own concern in my long life has been increasingly to emphasize this name and to say: 'in Him.' There is no salvation but in this name. In him is grace. In him is the spur to work, warfare, and fellowship. In him is all that I have attempted in my life in weakness and folly. It is there in him. I suggest then that we finish with Mozart as a sacred composer. I myself have always been very fond of the little *Missa Brevis in D Major,* again by the young Mozart. [In which they sing:] 'O Lamb of God, that takest away the sins of the world, have mercy upon us, grant us thy peace.'

— FINAL TESTIMONIES, 20-30

Karl Barth's lasting testimony is not to a new concept, to a new theology, to a dogma, or to a principle such as grace. Barth's lasting testimony is his faithful witness to Jesus Christ. This is what makes Karl Barth a great theologian—though he would certainly despise the term. It is not only his genius or his dedication to the truth but ultimately his determination to speak only that name, the name which is above all other names:

JESUS CHRIST

A BRIEF READING GUIDE

Now that I am done talking about Barth it is time you go and read him for yourself. Here I will recommend a reading plan for the *Church Dogmatics*, briefly describe some of Barth's most important works, as well as other primary works worth mentioning. I also recommend a few secondary sources by leading scholars which might be helpful for studying a particular subject more thoroughly.

Also please note that none of these books are in any particular order and that my recommendation is not a full endorsement of everything stated therein.

FIVE GREAT INTRODUCTORY BOOKS:

1. *Dogmatics in Outline*
— A short but profound introduction; one of the first books I'd recommend picking up to read for newcomers to Barth's theology.
2. *Evangelical Theology: An Introduction*
— One of Barth's final publications. I can't help but find it ironic how at the end of his life he decides to publish "an introduction" to evangelical theology, but that is exactly the spirit behind Barth's desire to always begin again at the beginning. This is another one of the books I'd first recommend to newcomers.

3. *Church Dogmatics* IV/1, §57 "The Work of God the Reconciler" and §58 "The Doctrine of Reconciliation (Survey)"

— This is the first 150 pages or so of volume IV/1; here you'll find a concise survey of Barth's doctrine of reconciliation well worth your attention. Read these pages and then re-read them again, here the major ideas of Barth's doctrine of reconciliation are all present. This is probably the best introduction for those willing to put in a bit of work.

4. *Deliverance to the Captives*

— Sermons to the Basel prison, part one.

5. *Barth in Conversation: Vol. 1, 1959-1962*

— This volume collects interviews, conversations, and Q&A sessions with Barth. He provides many frank, off-the-cuff responses to commonly asked questions about his work. It's an insightful and accessible book, but exceedingly helpful for newcomers to Barth's theology.

OTHER GREAT BOOKS:

1. *Christ and Adam: Man and Humanity in Romans 5*

2. *The Humanity of God*

— A short but important collection of lectures.

3. *The Epistle to the Romans*

— This is likely Barth's most famous book. While it is an exciting book to read and certainly well worth the effort, in my opinion, this is *not* a good introductory book. I wouldn't recommend it as the first book you pick up.

4. *Credo*

5. *Against the Stream*

— These are post-war lectures on the Church in the political sphere.

6. *Anselm: Fides Quaerens Intellectum*

— This book marked a drastic shifting-point in Barth's thought, forming the basis for much of *CD* II/1. Barth once said that he wished people paid more attention to this book since he considered it to be one of his most important.

7. *Göttingen Dogmatics*

— This was Barth's first attempt at dogmatics during his teaching position in Göttingen. Only the first volume has been translated into

English (presently), but there is talk of the complete set being available soon. It is an insightful look at Barth's early theology.

8. *Final Testimonies*

— A moving collection of Barth's final public remarks, which notably includes the beginning of an unfinished lecture he left mid-sentence on the night of his death.

9. *The Word of God and the Word of Man*

— The book which followed *Romans* and contains Barth's famous lecture on the "Strange New World Within the Bible."

10. *The Faith of the Church: A Commentary on the Apostles' Creed According to Calvin's Catechism*

11. *A Shorter Commentary on Romans*

12. *God in Action: Theological Addresses*

13. *Call for God*

— Part two of sermons to the Basel prisoners.

14. *Come, Holy Spirit: Sermons*

— An early collection of sermons presented together with Eduard Thurneysen.

15. *God's Search for Man*

— Another early collection of sermons, also with Thurneysen.

16. *The Christian Life: Lecture Fragments (Church Dogmatics, Vol. 4, Part 4)*

— This book is from lecture notes on Barth's unfinished volume IV/4.

17. *The Knowledge of God and the Service of God According to the Teaching of the Reformation*

— This may be of particular interest to those within the Reformed/Calvinist tradition.

18. *Church Dogmatics* (A Selection with Introduction by Helmut Gollwitzer)

— While I haven't used this volume myself, Gollwitzer was one of Barth's most important students. In this book, he has collected together some of the most notable sections from Barth's *Dogmatics*.

19. *Epistle to the Philippians*

— A relatively short commentary on Philippians from early lectures Barth taught shortly after the second edition of *Romans*.

20. *The Epistle to the Ephesians*

— Gathered from lectures given around the same time as the Philip-

pians commentary. Acts as another insightful look at Barth's early exeget-
ical work.

21. *The Holy Spirit and the Christian Life: The Theological Basis of Ethics*

HOW TO READ THE *CHURCH DOGMATICS?*

1. The first way I recommend to read Barth's *Dogmatics* is to begin
with the doctrine of reconciliation in volume IV. Not only do I think this
is Barth's most profound volume, but it has been rightly called a "mini-
dogmatics" in the midst of his *Dogmatics* because so much of Barth's most
important ideas are present. Reading this volume will never replace a
careful reading of the other significant volumes in *CD*, such as the
extremely important volume II, but it is an excellent introduction to what
Barth himself called the center of the Christian faith. This path would
certainly be a challenge for newcomers, but not an impossible one. The
benefit of jumping right in and reading Barth for yourself far out weights
the difficulty.

After reading volume IV I recommend reading volume II on the
doctrine of God, which contains the volumes which I think most drastically *shape* Barth's theology. After you've read these large volumes you'll
have a firm grip on Barth's thought and can continue on to volumes I and
III in whichever order you'd like. I don't mean to devalue the importance
of volumes I and III, but I have personally found the most helpful material from the *Dogmatics* to be found in volumes IV and II. A scholar
might tell you that every volume of the *Dogmatics* should be read in order,
but I am an amateur and can only speak to what I found to be the most
helpful as an amateur. Even today when I pick up a volume from the
Dogmatics it's far more likely that I will pick up a volume from IV or II
than from I or III.

2. Or why not just read Barth from the beginning? *CD* I/1 is a great place
to start, and Barth builds logically from there. If you dedicate yourself to
reading Barth why not dedicate yourself completely? If you're a consistent
reader it would only take a little over a year to finish—or sooner if you're
especially driven. I once heard that Wolfhart Pannenberg read the entire
Church Dogmatics in fewer than three months(!) in preparation to study in

Basel under Barth. You may stare up with fear at those fourteen thick volumes as if they were a theological Mount Everest, but it is not impossible to reach the summit when you dedicate yourself to a consistent reading schedule.

3. The final way to read Barth's *Church Dogmatics* is the way I read it. I jumped from volume to volume based on my interest in a particular subject. Feel free to do the same, to read in a random order based on what you're the most interested in. Use the outline of each volume I provided at the beginning of this book, start with what you are the most interested in Barth's theology, and then move on from there. This method helps you stay engaged with Barth more personally, and it was an enthralling experience for me to read in this way.

Barth often repeats himself, which some find tedious but I think it is extremely helpful for the reader. If you don't really "get" what Barth is saying the first time around, there will be another chance soon enough. So there is not an inherent *need* for you to read in chronological order. Barth always began again at the beginning, never presupposing anything but always working again with a continual focus on Jesus Christ. This makes his *Dogmatics* possible to read sporadically.

A few final comments about reading Barth's *Church Dogmatics*. It is best if you read as much as you can all at once. This may seem like a difficult thing to ask, but I made the initial mistake of reading only a few pages at a time, not reading again for several weeks, only to return having lost Barth's train of thought. Fifty pages are approximately how long it will take Barth to come full circle on any given subject. I would recommend trying to get through at least that much at a time, whether that's in a period of two or three consecutive days or one sitting.

Also, please don't fall to the temptation of skipping the small print. This is often the best section to get the clearest picture of what Barth is working towards. I made that mistake early on, but now I *savor* the small print. It is here that Barth is the most engaged with the Scriptures, with contemporary issues, and with other theologians or philosophers throughout history. At one point Barth thought to have these small print sections be the large print, and vice versa, because of how important these sections are. Don't skip them.

The small print often includes long quotes in Latin or Greek, which are impossible to understand if you are like me and can't read either language beyond a few phrases here or there. There are two ways you can solve this problem. The first is to use Google to look up a particular phrase or buy a theological dictionary to search through. This isn't necessarily the best way, but it's helped me from time to time. The better way is to get ahold of the T&T Clark study edition (in thirty-three volumes), which helpfully translates all of these phrases into English. This is the most expensive edition available, but you can purchase separate volumes individually if you have a particular section you need to study. This is the way I have typically solved this problem. I own the hardback edition in fourteen volumes which does not translate the Latin or Greek, but whenever I needed to study a particular volume I purchased the study edition of that section or relied on a Latin/Greek dictionary.

My final advice for reading Karl Barth is don't give up. The more you read, the more you'll get used to his difficult style. His sentences may be long and complex, but you'll soon get used to them. Don't be afraid of the initial difficulty it takes to read Barth. Go slow and engage with his thought process while you read. Think about what he is saying and why he is saying it. I can tell you from my own experience that while Barth at first seems impenetrable, he is not impossible. Just keep reading, and you'll get there.

Secondary works:

1. Robert Jenson's *Alpha and Omega* is a clear and concise study, specifically focused on Barth's doctrine of election, creation, the covenant, and nothingness.

2. Eberhard Jüngel's *God's Being Is in Becoming* is another excellent study, focusing on Barth's doctrine of God. Jüngel works through Barth's difficult idea that God's being is an *event*. It is challenging and dense, but well worth the effort.

3. Thomas F. Torrance's two books on Barth, *Karl Barth: An Introduction to His Early Theology* and *Karl Barth: Biblical and Evangelical Theologian*, are both excellent studies.

4. Eberhard Busch's *Karl Barth: His Life from Letters and Autobiograph-*

ical Texts and *The Great Passion: An Introduction to Karl Barth's Theology* are two helpful books written by Barth's final assistant in Basel. The first is widely considered to be Barth's unofficial auto-biography.

5. Arnold B. Come's *An Introduction to Barth's Dogmatics for Preachers* is a clear and helpful study, though I'd say its slightly underrated; Barth himself read it with approval.

6. George Hunsinger's *How to Read Karl Barth* is another classic; this book identifies six motifs that shape Barth's theology. Hunsinger is considered to be one of the leading living scholars of Barth's theology, alongside Bruce McCormack.

7. Hans Küng's *Justification* is a fascinating book connecting Barth's doctrine of justification with Catholic theology, which includes an insightful analysis of Barth's work.

8. Geoffrey W. Bromiley's *Introduction to the Theology of Karl Barth* is a running summary of Barth's *Church Dogmatics*. Bromiley was one of the primary editors and translators of *Church Dogmatics,* alongside Thomas F. Torrance.

9. Adam J. Johnson's *God's Being in Reconciliation* is a recent but fascinating study of Barth's doctrine of reconciliation, engaging Barth with the contemporary discussion of atonement theories.

10. *The Cambridge Companion to Karl Barth* is one of the best all-in-one, introductory collections, containing helpful essays on all of Barth's most important ideas. John Webster was the editor for this volume.

11. John B. Webster's *Karl Barth* is a clear and helpful study by an important scholar of Barth's work.

12. Hans Urs von Balthasar's *The Theology of Karl Barth* was an early study that met with Barth's approval, notable for challenging Barth's understanding of the *analogia entis* from the Catholic perspective.

13. G. C. Berkouwer's *The Triumph of Grace* is a fair but critical assessment of Barth's work.

14. Bruce McCormack and Clifford Anderson co-edited *Karl Barth and American Evangelicalism.* This book is a much-needed response to the negative assessments of Cornelius Van Til, and does a great job clearing the air of many of Van Til's slanderous false-claims about Barth's work.

15. *Karl Barth and Radical Politics* ed. by George Hunsinger. This includes an important early essay from Barth. We did not spend any time

on Barth's political thought, but it is well worth looking into. This text is the best to begin with.

16. *Karl Barth's Critically Realistic Dialectical Theology* by Bruce McCormack. This is a challenging book, but it is widely considered one of the best scholarly treatments of Barth's work.

WORKS CITED

Citations are listed chronologically and organized by chapter; citations have not been repeated with every usage.

Introduction:

God in Action; written by Karl Barth, edited and with an introduction by Elmer G. Homrighausen; Round Table Press, 1963.

Final Testimonies; written by Karl Barth, edited by Eberhard Busch, translated by Geoffrey W. Bromiley; William B. Eerdmans Publishing, 1977.

The Cambridge Companion to Karl Barth; edited by John Webster; Cambridge University Press, 2000.

Biography

The Word of God and the Word of Man; written by Karl Barth, forward and translation by Douglas Horton; Harper Publishing, 1957.

The Correspondences of Flannery O'Connor and the Brainerd Cheneys. Jackson, MS: University Press of Mississippi, 1986.

Chapter 1: Nein! to Natural Theology

How to Read Karl Barth: The Shape of His Theology; written by George Hunsinger; Oxford University Press, 1991.

God's Being Is in Becoming; written by Eberhard Jüngel, introduction and translation by John Webster; T&T Clark, 2001.

Karl Barth (Makers of Modern Theological Mind); written by David L. Mueller, edited by Bob E. Patterson; Word Books Publisher, 1972.

Evangelical Theology: An Introduction; written by Karl Barth, translated by Grover Foley; William B. Eerdmans Publishing, 1963.

The Epistle to the Romans; written by Karl Barth, translated from the sixth edition by Edwyn C. Hoskyns; Oxford University Press, 1968.

The Triumph of Grace in the Theology of Karl Barth; written by G. C. Berkouwer; William B. Eerdmans Publishing, 1956.

Come Holy Spirit: Sermons; written by Karl Barth and Eduard Thurneysen, translated by George Richards, Elmer G. Homrighausen, and Karl Ernst; Wipf and Stock Publishers, 2009.

Chapter 2: The Triune God of Revelation

Karl Barth: An Introduction to His Early Theology 1910-1931; written by Thomas F. Torrance; T&T Clark, 2004.

Dogmatics in Outline; written by Karl Barth, translated by G. T. Thomson; Harper & Row Publishers, 1959.

The Christian Doctrine of God, One Being Three Persons; written by Thomas F. Torrance; T&T Clark, 1996.

God's Search for Man; written by Karl Barth and Eduard Thurneysen, translated by George Richards, Elmer G. Homrighausen, and Karl Ernst; Round Table Press, 1935.

Chapter 3: The Threefold Word of God

An Introduction to Barth's Dogmatics *for Preachers*; written by Arnold B. Come; The Westminster Press, 1963.

Introduction to the Theology of Karl Barth; written by Geoffrey W. Bromiley; William B. Eerdmans Publishing, 1979.

The Göttingen Dogmatics Volume I: Instruction in the Christian Religion;

written by Karl Barth, edited by Hannelotte Reiffen, translated by Geoffrey W. Bromiley; William B. Eerdmans Publishing, 1991.

Homiletics; written by Karl Barth, translated by Geoffrey W. Bromiley and Donald E. Daniels; Westminster / John Knox Press, 1991.

Chapter 4: There is No Hidden God Behind the Back of Jesus Christ

Covering Up Luther: How Barth's Christology Challenged the Deus Absconditus *that Haunts Modernity*; written by Rustin E. Brian; Cascade Books, 2013.

Chapter 5: The God of Election

Alpha and Omega: A Study in the Theology of Karl Barth; written by Robert W. Jenson; Wipf and Stock Publishers, 2002.

The Humanity of God; written by Karl Barth, translated by John Newton Thomas and Thomas Wieser; John Knox Press, 1996.

Karl Barth and American Evangelicalism; edited by Bruce L. McCormack and Clifford B. Anderson; William B. Eerdmans Publishing, 2011.

Deliverance to the Captives; written by Karl Barth, preface by John Marsh, translated by Marguerite Wieser; Harper & Row Publishers, 1978.

Chapter 6: Creation and the Covenant

Christ and Adam: Man and Humanity in Romans 5; written by Karl Barth, introduced by Wilhelm Pauck, translated by T. A. Smail; Collier Books, 1962.

Justification: The Doctrine of Karl Barth and a Catholic Reflection; written by Hans Küng, with a letter to the author by Karl Barth, translated by Thomas Collins, Edmund E. Tolk, and David Granskou; Westminster John Knox Press, 2004.

Call for God; written by Karl Barth, translated by A. T. Mackay; Harper & Row Publishers, 1967.

Chapter 7: Reconciliation

Karl Barth: His Life from Letters and Autobiographical Texts; written by Eberhard Busch, translated by John Bowden; Fortress Press, 1976.

God's Being in Reconciliation: The Theological Basis of the Unity and Diversity of the Atonement in the Theology of Karl Barth; written by Adam J. Johnson; Bloomsbury T&T Clark, 2012.

Chapter 8: The Church and Ethics

The Analogy of Grace: Karl Barth's Moral Theology; written by Gerald McKenny; Oxford University Press, 2010.

The Holy Spirit and the Christian Life: The Theological Basis of Ethics; written by Karl Barth, foreword by Robin W. Lovin, translated by R. Birch Hoyle; Westminster / John Knox Press, 1993.

Against the Stream: Shorter Post-War Writings, 1946-53 written by Karl Barth; SCM Press, 1954.

Karl Barth and Radical Politics, Second Edition; written and edited by George Hunsinger; Cascade Books, 2017.

ABOUT THE AUTHOR

STEPHEN D. MORRISON is a prolific American writer, ecumenical theologian, novelist, artist, and literary critic. A strong sense of creativity and curiosity drives his productive output of books on a wide range of subjects.

This book is the third in his "Plain English Series." Previous volumes include *Karl Barth in Plain English* and *T. F. Torrance in Plain English*.

For more on Stephen, please visit his website. There you can stay up to date with his latest projects and ongoing thoughts.

WWW.SDMORRISON.ORG

ALSO BY STEPHEN D. MORRISON

Plain English Series:

Karl Barth in Plain English (2017)

T. F. Torrance in Plain English (2017)

Jürgen Moltmann in Plain English (2018)

Schleiermacher in Plain English (forthcoming)

For a complete list of the projected volumes in this series, please visit:
www.SDMorrison.org/plain-english-series/

Other titles:

Welcome Home: The Good News of Jesus (2016)

10 Reasons Why the Rapture Must be Left Behind (2015)

We Belong: Trinitarian Good News (2015)

Where Was God?: Understanding the Holocaust in the Light of God's Suffering
(2014)